"John's text distills the concepts of Bert on Method into one comprehensive volum to understand and unravel issues of national str in our world today. Accessible to the novice and *he Healing of Individuals, Families and Nations* should be a valuable addition to the library of work dedicated to healing our ancestral lineage."
—Jamy Faust, Hellinger Boston

"As a colleague I congratulate John Payne on his excellent book. Not only does it provide a profound introduction to the world of Family Constellations but it also demonstrates to all of us how we are touched by turmoil in the real world, both in the past and now. The book reveals both the roots of, and some solutions to, conflicts between nations and races."
—Dr. Bertold Ulsamer, author of *The Art and Practice of Family Constellations*

"*The Healing of Individuals, Families and Nations* is not just another systemic family constellation book; it is a gift of profound insight, wisdom, and love. To a lay person, John Payne's choice of words and his clear explanations are masterful, making it "easy friendly" for the reader to ponder this unrestricted matrix—that is, without boundaries, an open state of presence in the moment. Payne invites his readers to allow themselves to be moved and to partake of the different deep textures, participating to look together at what has not been seen about one's own family contradictions, then to move toward kindness and respond freely to cease excluding the other.

"Through the author's transparency, we find the courage to look at fear and hatred in our own systems, cultures, nations. To look at images of the enemy, the "evil doers" that inspire hatred and outrage and breed further contempt. We are taken to witness and explore, collectively, how this hate focuses on—and excludes—an individual or an entire culture or political ideology. We then are taken towards profound healing. Payne's book reawakens long suppressed ways of being that may help "fields of conflict" become "fields of wisdom" and contribute to surprising reconciliation and peace.

"John Payne invites us to listen to the whole of what is expressed, and through this find ourselves free, not obliged to do anything, nor say anything, nor even come to any conclusions. A book long overdue. I thank him."
—Drindy AidaLinda Keller, Director of the Bert Hellinger Institute, Florida

The Healing
of Individuals,
Families and Nations

By John L. Payne

FINDHORN
Press

© John L. Payne 2005

First published by Findhorn Press 2005

ISBN 1-84409-066-3

British Library Cataloguing-in-Publication Data.
A catalogue record for this book is available from the British Library.

Edited by Shari Mueller
Illustrations by Sandy Brück
Cover design by Damian Keenan
Interior design by Pam Bochel
Printed and bound by WS Bookwell, Finland

Published by
Findhorn Press
305A The Park,
Findhorn, Forres
Scotland IV36 3TE

Tel 01309 690582
Fax 01309 690036
email: info@findhornpress.com

www.findhornpress.com

TABLE OF CONTENTS

INTRODUCTION

I first attended Family Constellations given by my dear friend and colleague, Annebiene Pilon, in Rotterdam in late 1998. On first hearing of this work I was admittedly quite sceptical, not understanding how 'representation' was going to be any different from 'role play' or how this way of working was going to be useful when none of the people knew me or my story. However, I was to learn very quickly that our stories, aside from clear facts concerning specific events, had no place in this new and exciting modality. On my first attendance at a workshop, I was amazed, and indeed a little frightened, with the depth of the process, its accuracy, and how the true underlying dynamic of a family is revealed. At the time, I had not spoken to my parents for a while owing to issues that had surfaced in other therapies I had been employing. With time, the gulf that existed between us closed, and I was able to start the healing process once again, this time with much greater insight, understanding and compassion. Like most therapists, I came from what I considered to be a highly dysfunctional family to a point in my life when I could see clearly that through becoming a therapist, I was simply trying to find solutions for my own life. This level of honesty with myself brought great liberation, enabling me to be of greater service to others.

Since those early beginnings back in 1999, I have attended countless workshops, benefited from training and coaching, and have myself given more than 100 Family Constellations workshops. This in itself has been a journey, one that will never cease to deeply move me, inspire me, encourage me and teach me about the realm of human relationships and the Soul. Additionally, I cannot talk of Family Constellation work without mentioning Bert Hellinger, a renowned German psychotherapist who is the originator of this profound body of work. His books and seminars have been a great inspiration to me and form the basis of my own adventure into the realm of human relationships.

My intention with this book is to share with you a glimpse into a world that goes beyond our everyday perceptions of what is true and our analysis of what we suppose to be the cause of our limiting, disruptive life patterns and illnesses. Through the pages of this book, you will begin to see yourself not simply as an individual, but as someone who belongs to the greater Soul of a family, an ethnic group and a nation, each of which has a direct impact not only on the way in which we live our lives, but also on our emotional, physical and spiritual health and well-being. I encourage you to spend time with each story that has been told in these pages and monitor your own physical and emotional reactions, for I have found that the body never lies, and much of your own story will be discovered in this way.

What this work reveals quite simply is that our feelings may not be our own and that we can be entangled in the fate of others, living their lives, instead of being in contact with the essence of our own unique Soul. Both seasoned psychotherapists and traditional healers are amazed by the efficiency of this work. My intention is to offer this body of work to you in a way that is devoid of psychotherapeutic jargon so that the greater significance can be felt and experienced by anyone looking for insights.

> With Love,
> John L. Payne

ACKNOWLEDGEMENTS

Firstly, I need to acknowledge Bert Hellinger for having brought Family Constellation work to the world as a gift from his Soul. His innovative pioneering approach to the world of family dynamics and the field of human relationships has ushered in a new era when rapid solutions can be found to the most complex of human problems. Secondly, my dearly beloved friend Annebiene Pilon in the Netherlands, a professional, highly skilled, shining light in this field of work. I am indebted to her for her counsel, teaching, support, love and friendship. Additionally, other teachers and colleagues have crossed my path, all of whom have contributed greatly to my insights and experience, namely: Peter Adriaan de Vries and Gabrielle Borkan. A very special mention must go to Drindy Keller, Director of the Bert Hellinger Institute, Florida, U.S.A. Thank you for opening so many doors for me, for your love, friendship and support. Also, my deep gratitude goes out to Hilda de la Rosa, a profound and highly skilled teacher in her own right, a dear friend, impeccable advisor and an inspiration to many, not least myself. Thank you, Hilda!

A special thank you must also go to students, friends and associates that have supported my work in so many valuable ways: Hilda de la Rosa, Colleen Joy-Page, Robert Howes, Frauke Mascali, all of whom have shown great generosity, plus Verity Meyer, Di du Preez, Allyson Logan, Jonathan Atkinson, Rashnee Parhanse, Karin Huyssen, Pam Roux, Lorato Scherpenhuizen, Karen Lange, Bev Moss, Dr. Newton Kondaveti, Dr. Lakshmi Kondaveti, Dr. Delia Robertson, Winnie Kyriakides, Sonja Simak, plus my many clients and also the many students from the Academy of Metaphysics in Johannesburg. Thank you!

Last but not least, my deepest gratitude goes to Willie Engelbrecht, my life partner and good friend. Thank you for all of your support and for believing in me even at times when I didn't believe in myself. You have been a light in my life!

With Love,
John L. Payne

In Memory of My Mother

Lourdes Clemencia Bebeagua

1934 – 2004
Gibraltar

CHAPTER ONE

THE ORDERS OF LOVE

The Orders of Love describe a natural hierarchy that has been observed through the practice of Family Constellations. What we have observed is that there is a distinct order that states who belongs, and who doesn't belong not only to a family system, but also to groups and nations. On working with individuals, we observe that each of us has three levels of conscience: firstly, the conscience we have as individuals which dictates to us what is right and wrong, our responsibilities, and our reactions to certain conditions; additionally, we belong to the collective conscience of our biological family, the connections and influence of which can span many generations; and lastly, we participate in the conscience of our ethnic and national groups—be that Jewish, Afrikaans, Xhosa, Zulu, White, Black, Coloured, Muslim, Hindu, Catholic, Protestant, English, German or Scottish, etc.

In observing work with clients during the process of Family Constellations, we see an undeniable and almost measurable effect when the Orders of Love have been disrupted in some families. The Orders of Love prescribe who comes first, who belongs after that, and describes a natural flow of love from grandparents, to parents and to children. These orders span countless generations but tend to be experienced as having the greatest influence within three to seven generations. So how do the Orders of Love become disrupted? As these ancient orders dictate who belongs and how, disruptions take place when individuals or groups have been excluded, either deliberately or as a result of family members not being able to embrace the difficult fate of another family member. The overriding principle of the Orders of Love is that parents give life, and that children receive life. Therefore, when a child—no matter the age—is motivated to place himself above a parent, or equal to a parent, there are consequences in terms of the natural flow of the Orders of Love towards him. The cost to the child with such posturing is usually evident in disruptive life patterns.

The most common disruptions are caused by the early death of a parent or grandparent, the death of a child, miscarriages, abortions, an individual being ousted from a family in the role of 'black sheep', or if a murder or other

1

injustice has taken place. All of these events can be felt and observed to have a deep residual impact on our lives today, even when they have taken place three, four or five generations back. On encountering these ancient Orders of Love, seasoned therapists are not only amazed by the efficiency of working within this new concept, but are also humbled by the power of working in this innovative and fresh way, inspiring them to find new solutions for clients that have hitherto eluded them.

When we look closer at the Orders of Love, we enter a realm that is beyond traditional psychotherapy, and initiates a movement to cross the threshold into the dominion of the Soul. The Soul by its very nature is equal to, and inclusive of, all things. At the heart of the Soul is the acknowledgement and acceptance of what is. This is the basis and power of love. Through this nature of love, we become liberated to belong without entanglement in the fate of others, as well as from a collective conscience that may be detrimental to us in terms of creating disruptive life patterns. Resolutions for interruptions in the natural Orders of Love lie in seeing each member of our family (or nation) as belonging equally, regardless of circumstances: whether they are strong or weak, amicable or argumentative, mentally or physically handicapped, committed suicide or died at a very young age. In restoring the Orders of Love, we need to allow and respect the fate of each member of our family (or nation), no matter how burdensome that fate may be, for each individual must be able to be strengthened not only by their fate, but also by any responsibility that they may have for it. What has been observed time and time again, is that disruptive life patterns—be they manifest as physical illness or difficulties in relationships—can be attributed to an interruption in the Orders of Love, as well as to the difficulty that some individuals have in allowing the fate of another to remain where it is, instead of taking it on as their own. Often, in working to restore the Orders of Love through Family Constellations, the client has little or no conscious awareness of his entanglements with the fate of others, but when revealed through a constellation, he becomes acutely aware of his hidden loyalties and begins to consciously defend them.

The Orders of Love rarely exist intact within the average family. When members of a family cause a disruption to the Orders of Love—albeit this is more often than not realised or responded to in an unconscious way and not acknowledged—the awareness does not simply fade away from the family conscience or Soul; it remains intact. If an individual has been ousted unfairly from a family, another family member—even several generations later—will be compelled to restore balance and order by suffering a similar fate out of unspoken loyalty. It is in the same way that nations or national and ethnic groups that have been victims of other groups go on to imitate the original perpetrators. Victims and perpetrators share a fate with one another and when the victim is denied or excluded in some way, the perpetrator is also excluded—given a status that is less than human—compelling future generations to take on as their own the fate of either the perpetrator or the victim. When we look at perpetrators, it must be remembered that there is much more to the individual than that moment in time when he becomes the murderer or persecutor. His being is much larger than a single event, and it is the totality of his being rather than a single event that defines who he is. Let me share some examples:

Although raised in a Christian household, a client was compelled to convert to Judaism. On exploring family history, we see that his great-grandfather left his wife for a Jewish woman and had a child with her. This child, Jewish owing to its mother, was excluded, not acknowledged as a brother to the client's grandfather, not acknowledged as an uncle or great-uncle by the client or his family. This constitutes an exclusion which creates disruption in the Orders of Love; therefore, as the nature of the Soul is inclusion and to be equal to all things, the client feels compelled to share in the fate of his great-uncle and live with the consequences of conversion to Judaism within the context of belonging to a Christian family.

In this way, we as children, and our own children, take on the energies and feelings of ancestors, living life as if they themselves were a particular ancestor who had been forgotten or ousted in some way. By far the most common entanglement and disruption to the Orders of Love are observed when there has been the early death of an individual within a family, be it a parent or a child. When an individual dies early, it is very difficult for surviving family members to accept the fate of that person; this is particularly so for parents who lose an infant, or for a young child when a parent dies. When we are unable to look at and fully acknowledge the dead, they, too, become excluded, for their fate has been rejected. Fate is a matter for the Soul.

A client reports that she has often struggled with suicidal feelings and has been on a life-long search for spiritual truth. On working with her family, we learned that her mother's sister died just a few hours after birth. The child was neither named nor given a funeral and was never spoken of, a clearly taboo subject within the family. On setting up her constellation, the client immediately wept when looking at the representative for the dead child and reported, "It feels as if I've been looking for her all of my life." The client also reported feeling guilty simply for being alive, and now she had a clear understanding why.

My client was compelled to represent the dead child in some way, and to share in its fate through not being fully present in life, with one foot in the grave, so to speak. When a child dies, the parents often cannot look at the child, and are unable to accept the child as their own, thus the child becomes ousted from the family. In such cases, even four or five generations later, the effect can be felt and the children and grandchildren of later generations can feel compelled to share the fate of such a child in some way, either through action, or by carrying the feelings. More often than not, clients who report being on a life-long quest for spiritual truth or 'something', are usually looking for someone who has died and been forgotten.

So how do we work with the Orders of Love and access the information that is revealed? We do so by employing what we have come to call the Knowing Field.

The Knowing Field

In Family Constellation work we use representatives to stand in for members of our family and ancestors; this is when we engage the unseen presence that we have come to know as the Knowing Field. It is then that we meet the phenomenon that representatives have access to information and feelings of the individuals they are representing. This, for the representatives, can be a powerful and life-changing experience in its own right as they step into another's shoes and 'become' someone else, with little to no knowledge of the personality and circumstances of the individual they are representing.

During a constellation process, a representative is asked to stand in for the client's grandfather. On being placed in position, the representative lifts up one foot and rests it behind the knee of his other leg, therefore standing on one leg. The client gasps and utters, "My grandfather lost his leg in Wolrd War I!"

Everyone taking part in Family Constellations for the first time is amazed, deeply touched and altered in some way by means of their exposure to what they see unfolding before them, as well as by their own often intense experiences when asked to represent a complete stranger. On hearing about this work, the reactions are often sceptical, even incredulous, some wondering if it could possibly be true, some adding conjecture that representatives are merely acting out of a need to create healing or resolution for a client. However, sometimes what a representative feels and expresses is far from loving and none of the feelings of any of the representatives can be predicted in advance. What we do hear frequently are statements from clients like, "That's just like my brother—that is what he would say." There is a certain sense of mystery as to how this happens, for the representatives are not required to be psychically gifted, but are ordinary people attending a workshop. We hear time and again from participants verifying the truth of the feelings, attitudes and events that are being represented. In some way, the representatives are either absorbing the energy of the family Soul, or simply becoming part of it—which is astounding in its own right—but the true power of the work comes from releasing the mystery of it, accepting what is, and simply using the Knowing Field as expressed through the representatives in order to bring order to chaos and resolution to disharmony.

Setting up the Knowing Field

There is no particular procedure for setting up the Knowing Field, it simply comes to life through both the intention of the client to work with her family, an issue or a theme in her life, or the intention of the therapist to work in this way. In most cases, the client chooses representatives from workshop attendees and places them in a standing pattern that has meaning to her, representing a picture of how the family feels for her, within the constellation floor space. However, at times, the therapist will choose someone randomly, adding to the constellation by bringing in representatives for grandparents or other more distant family members. Almost instantaneously, the individual selected becomes a part of the story with all the associated feelings. Very often, mostly in order to test a hunch, a representative will be chosen by the therapist without being told who or what he represents. The results are identical: other representatives respond to him, and they themselves become a part of the constellation with all of the feelings, accessing in the same way knowledge and feelings that are known to the actual family members, even though they may not be present.

Recounting this phenomenon does not explain how it works, but is a mere description of what has been observed and the benefits of working within the scope of the Knowing Field. What is very clear is that when both therapist and workshop attendees are able to submit to the mystery, simply accepting what is, then the full benefits and power of this work can be enjoyed as we move away from being astounded and simply take it for granted that this is how it is, and that it works. The most appropriate stance is simply to stand back with respect that the Knowing Field belongs to something that is far greater than ourselves and that we don't need to understand it intellectually in order to befriend it.

Revelations of the Knowing Field

The Knowing Field simply reveals the energies present within a family, it cannot be used to establish facts or evidence for given events. However, often within a family constellation, family secrets or events hitherto unknown by the client, are later confirmed. When working with the field, we have to be very aware of the interconnectedness of all members of a family, spanning many generations.

During a constellation, a representative for the client feels traumatised by the death of a school friend, re-living the scene of the accident. The client then also states that he has similar feelings, although has no recollection of the accident that took place. After speaking with family members, the client verifies that it was his brother who was at the scene of the accident, not himself.

This example illustrates how the 'energies' of events can be felt by many, but the facts can either be distorted, or highly accurate, belonging to someone else, or even to an entirely different generation of the same family. Is using the Knowing Field in this way unreliable? Yes, it is unreliable when our sole motive is to look for facts, but if our motive is to find resolution for disharmony, then the Knowing Field can be trusted, tested and relied upon when we don't make assumptions. However, having said all this, with Family Constellations we are frequently pointed towards unknown facts which later come to light and are confirmed.

An Afrikaans client had felt troubled with her son's depressed nature and troublesome, often aggressive behaviour. On setting up the constellation, the representative for her son looked accusingly at his father. The client revealed that her husband had served in the army on the border with Angola as part of an anti-terrorist campaign. With this information, I took three individuals to represent the Angolans, one of whom immediately laid down on the floor as if dead. The son's representative felt compelled to move across the room to stand with the

Angolans, sharing in their fate. The representative of the father could not look at the Angolans, was irritated by his son standing with them, and looked away.

This constellation in no way proves that the father had committed atrocities or was involved in war crimes, but it does tell us that the father, one way or another, has not come to terms with his experiences and has excluded the 'enemy' and his involvement in some way. The son and his compulsion to represent the Angolans is testimony to the Orders of Love which state 'that which is denied or excluded, will be represented by another'. The resolution to this is to have the son stand with his father and say, "Respectfully, Father, I leave this with you," or perhaps, "No matter what your past is, you are still my father, and I am still your son." These simple but very powerful sentences are known as Healing Sentences.

Healing Sentences

Healing Sentences are the language of the Soul. They are simple, express truth, and acknowledge what is. The power of the healing sentences lies in their simplicity, as they move us from the story and opinion, to simply stating what is undeniable. Over the years—collectively and individually— facilitators of Family Constellations have developed standard healing sentences that have been proven to have a healing effect. However, at times, the Knowing Field informs us and provides us with the appropriate sentence. This occurs when the facilitator has emptied his or her mind, released expectation and the need to fix anything, and is simply open with deep respect towards the family. With this neutral approach, the facilitator is often able to hear the words expressed by the field, and at times, the words are expressed spontaneously through a representative. There is a world of difference between the practice of psychodrama and the use of healing sentences within Family Constellations. The basis of this work is simple truth and acknowledging what is, whereas psychodrama, like much psychotherapy, tends towards creating and becoming stuck in stories which often ignore simple truths, creating a view of reality that is neither helpful nor healing.

Here are some typical healing sentences that have been observed to create a healing movement within clients and their family system:

On early death of a sibling

It's a great pity that you couldn't stay, because I've missed you.

Look upon me kindly me if I stay.

Bless me if I live life fully, in honour of you.

Wait patiently for me, I shall come when it's my proper time, and not one moment before.

Parents to children when an infant has died

It was so difficult when you left; I could no longer look at you.

Now that we've given a place to your brother once more, we can see you.

In the case of divorce

It's a pity that things went the way that they did. I take all that was good between us and give it a place in my heart.

I honour the part of you that I see alive in our children.

I honour the part of your father that I see alive in you dear Son, and it is good to see.

Thank you for the gift of our children; without you, I would not have this blessing.

These are just a few examples of healing sentences that have been tried and tested and have been found to be very effective. Other healing sentences will be introduced later in the book. The important role of healing sentences cannot be underestimated. Unlike traditional forms of therapy, Family Constellations looks at the bare facts and is event-orientated, in other words, we ask "What happened?" rather than "How do you feel?" Often, in traditional psychotherapy—although it, too, has its place in the healing process—clients can become embroiled in their own story, a story which is subjective rather than objective. Most therapists would agree that if you were to ask several children from the same family to describe their experience of their parents, we could at times assume that each of the siblings was in fact from a different family and not related at all. This is the power of subjective stories; they create our perception and then our experience of reality. When working with individuals within the context of Family Constellations, we do not need to know, nor is it desirable to know, the personalities of the individuals being represented. Statements like, "My brother was the favourite" or "My mother was controlling" or "My father was distant" do not support the system of using representatives within the Knowing Field and getting a true picture of any given family or situation. Instead, we ask about events and the known facts of the family. For example:

- The early death of parents and grandparents
- The death of an infant or someone young
- Accidental deaths and murders
- Abortions, miscarriages and stillbirths
- Adoptions
- Anyone who has been forced into the role of black sheep or is considered to be the black sheep of the family
- War experiences
- The experiences of ancestors, such as the American Civil War, Anglo-Boer War, Apartheid, the Holocaust, the Pogroms, Native American and Australian Aboriginal Genocide, African Slavery and the Diaspora, WWII and other wars
- Divorce
- Previous significant relationships such as former spouse or first love
- Ill-gotten gain

With this information, we can anticipate possible problem areas and interruptions to the Orders of Love and on that basis add various elements to a constellation based on the information gained from the client. Then, and only then, can we observe, through the representatives, which events the client is entangled with, in terms of making the fate of another part of the client's own life experience. Working in this way, we are reminded of the Biblical sentence, "The sins of the father will be visited upon the son", as we observe how the events of the past mould how we live our lives today.

Common Events and Their Impact

In working with Family Constellations and the Knowing Field, there are certain events that display common patterns and are to be witnessed in most constellations. One of the objectives of working with Family Constellations is to identify systemic entanglements. These entanglements are defined as when one individual becomes entwined in the events of the past, thereby experiencing and feeling the fate of another as his own.

Early Death of a Sibling

The early death of a sibling, whether as stillbirth, infant, child, or teenager, often places a burden on the surviving brothers and sisters. They often feel a draw towards death and a sense of guilt for having lived, *even when the child dies before they were born.* At times we observe that one of the parents—usually the mother—has a strong pull to be with the dead child, such is the power of maternal instincts. When this occurs another child may step forward as if to say, "I'll go, so that you can stay with the other children." What we have observed many times is that the living children have no sense of their place in the world or where they belong. When a child dies young, the living children perceive themselves to be one of three children, when in fact they are one of four children. When we observe the Orders of Love, we experience that natural hierarchy is important for the free flowing of love. In other words, if a client is considered the firstborn, but in fact there was a sibling before her who had died young, the true firstborn is excluded. Not only do we observe a pull from someone else to share in the fate of the dead child, but our client is also misplaced within the hierarchy of the family.

On placing her mother's two stillborn children in a constellation in right order, a client exclaimed, "That's a relief! I'm no longer the eldest and I no longer feel the need to be extra perfect to make up for those who are missing. It feels good to be the third child!"

Early Death of a Parent

When a parent dies when his children are still young, it is not only difficult for the spouse to accept her fate, but also for the children to accept theirs. The child often feels abandoned and angry at the parent for leaving him this way. This in turn leads to the child excluding his parent, refusing to accept not only the fate of his parent's death, but also his own fate as a child who has lost a parent. In addition to his own feelings of longing to be with his deceased parent, when the child becomes an adult and has children of his own, they can be drawn towards their mother, father, grandmother or grandfather...drawn towards the dead and feeling compelled to represent a grandparent who has been excluded through the denial and non-acceptance of her fate. Working with such cases is deeply moving and much healing and resolution can be found through accessing the Knowing Field within the context of a family constellation.

Often, the surviving spouse feels resentment at the death of the other parent, excluding him from her heart, and one of the children replaces him.

My father died when I was eight years old; from that point onwards I became my mother's husband—in a way, the head of the household. I was no longer a child, but a friend and confidant to my mother. It has been difficult for me to sustain relationships with other women.

When a child takes the place of a missing parent, not only does he no longer have access to the energies of the departed parent—therefore his sense of belonging may well be absent—but he also finds it difficult to move out of the sphere of influence of the living parent. In the case of a boy who has lost his father at an early age, it is difficult for him to belong to the world of men, as he has remained in the sphere of influence of his mother for so long. Additionally, on entering adult relationships, he is not truly free to love a spouse as he is already, in a sense, involved in a spousal relationship with his mother.

Divorce

When working with divorced couples or individuals, especially when there are children, it is important to bring a client to a point where he can remember the original love that he felt for his spouse. What we commonly see in divorce, is that children, although possibly having physical access to the other parent, often do not feel free to love their father or mother fully, out of loyalty to the parent who perceives himself as the injured party. In this way, children become embroiled in the private affairs of their parents and very often a child then takes the place of the missing parent which does not allow him to be free. Part of the power of using the Knowing Field through setting up a family constellation, is that the client is able to see clearly—without masks, pretence or justification—the effect that her particular stance is having upon her children. When divorced couples act in ways that are detrimental to children, they do so out of hurt...hurt and pain for a love that once was. Through this work, we can take divorced parents to a place where they remember the love that they had for one another, and the moments when their children were conceived in love. In essence, when dealing with divorce, the true power of Family Constellation work is the power of love, coupled with unwavering truth and compassion.

A young man in his late thirties attended a workshop desperate to find solutions for his failing, new marriage. After just two years his young wife was asking for a divorce. On setting up a constellation for his family of origin, it was very clear that he was not free from the influence of his mother, and his representative stood by her side, unable to look at his father. On asking the representative why he couldn't look at his father he replied, "It would be disloyal to my mother." The client nodded in agreement.

In this particular case, this young man had no access to his father and did not feel free to leave his mother's side; therefore, he was not able to fully take a wife, for in a sense, he already had a wife in the form of his mother. When young men or women do not feel connected to the parent of the same gender, they have no access to the energies that we may describe as 'the world of men' or the 'world of women'. In cultures where there are no specific rituals that bestow the rights of passage on young people into the world of adulthood, these rights of passage are passed on in more subtle ways, primarily through social and emotional contact with the parent of the same gender. Often in this work we have observed that there is great inner strength to be gained from the energies of our ancestors. When a young man is not connected to his father, the giver of life, he is denied access to the strength of the male line; the same is true for a woman who has no access to her mother. What is very significant is that equal importance and respect is given to both the world of men and the world of women. For each has its own unique experience and source of strength, as well as sharing much common experience.

No matter the circumstances of the divorce, whether it was a result of alcoholism, physical violence or an extra-marital affair, it is important not to lose sight of the gift of a child who was given as a result of the original love that existed between the couple. When one parent dishonours the other and denies the gift, the child is shamed in the process, and this in turn weakens the child, so much so, that he may not be able to sustain loving and lasting relationships in adult life. It is much more complex than assuming that a child will simply imitate the patterns of his parents, creating a divorce as they did. The greater influence is the child's access to energies of the parent, and in the case of a father, that is life, and the mother, the origin of love. For fathers are the beginning of life, and mothers the origin of love. When access to these fundamental energies is blocked or denied, our lives become disruptive and unsatisfactory.

Emotional Incest

The occurrence of *emotional incest* is far more common than physical incest; however, the effect upon us can be just as devastating, as it is devoid of the taboo that society places upon sexual incest, the guilt and shame is far less, but still noticeable. Emotional incest takes place when a parent has her primary emotional relationship with one of the children, instead of with her spouse. This can take the form of taking a child into confidence, speaking to the child as a friend, and placing a child in a supportive role. This occurs more frequently when a marriage has broken down, or one parent leaves, or a spouse dies early.

My parents were no longer getting along and my father took my bedroom and I slept with my mother from age nine until I was about fifteen. Every time I wanted to date someone, or enter into a new relationship, I felt guilty for abandoning my mother and felt that I had no right to love and respect my father. I miss my father dearly.

It is not necessary for a parent to take a child into her bed for emotional incest to take place. The simple act of taking a child into confidence and treating a child like a friend is sufficient to cause harm. The harm is done as the child will never be able to meet the parent's expectations, having been given an emotional responsibility that is far beyond his capabilities. Additionally, the child will perceive the parent as weak and in need of assistance. This can be a life-long relationship of bondage, not allowing the child to be free to form his own deep and lasting, intimate relationships. Through the process of Family Constellations, we can see that the parent who relies on a child in such ways, is herself weakened by events that took place in her own family of origin. Through restructuring in a family constellation, the child can then begin the process of freeing himself from bondage. However, in most cases such as these, there is much resistance on the part of the client to untangle himself in this way, as his bond of loyalty is very strong. However, when viewed from the perspective of how it is creating disruptions in his own adult relationships, the resistance beings to fade. A powerful healing sentence would be used in such cases, "I am just your child, you are the big one, I am just the little one."

Sexual Abuse and Incest

Owing to the great taboo that is placed upon incest and sexual abuse, great damage is done not only by society as a whole, but also by therapists who seek to polarise the parties into that of victim and perpetrator. Most of us have either shared or have been witness to the sentiment that all child molesters need to be punished severely, even put to death. So what happens with the child? When society postures itself with such aggression towards those who sexually abuse children, what is impressed upon the child is that something terrible has happened; the net effect of that is that the shame of the child is deepened. In my observation, most of the feelings associated with abuse such as guilt, shame, self-loathing and suicidal tendencies take form and shape *well after* the sexual abuse has taken place and are a direct result of adult reaction to such a taboo subject.

I was consumed with hatred for my brother, I only had to think of him and my skin crawled with disgust. My parents had disowned him and therefore I felt justified in hating him in this way. However, when you had me say, "I allowed it out of love for you." I was first horrified that you would ask me to say such a thing, but as I repeated the healing sentence, I felt overwhelmed with love for him. Suddenly I could truly feel what you were saying and that for my part, the love was sweet and innocent and in that moment, all of the years and layers of shame simply fell away. I no longer felt ashamed to say out loud that I love my brother. I had felt obliged to hate him.

In working with many cases of sexual abuse within a family or close relatives, we have observed that it is only when the child is free to feel the virtue of her love for another, that she once again gains her innocence and is free of the shackles of shame, guilt and self-loathing.

When a daughter is sexually abused by her own father, we place a great burden upon the child when she is denied the right to love him. A child's loyalty to a parent is almost unbreakable, and when she is obliged by society and other family members to hate him, we have observed that she will sabotage many good things in her life—such as career and relationships—in order to pay a sense of penance for her disloyalty. Family members and therapists will often worsen this situation on observing these disruptive life patterns by further vilifying the father. This, in turn, creates a deeper polarisation between victim and perpetrator, often forcing the child to punish herself even more in order to create some sense of balance. What is often ignored in cases of incest is the hidden guilty one or ones. This is often the mother and her role.

What we observe frequently through the process of family constellations and the use of the Knowing Field, is that the mother has in some way turned away from the father, and at times, freely offers up her daughter as a replacement. This offering up of a daughter as a replacement is rarely conscious as a deliberate act of offering a child as a sexual partner. It occurs when the attention of a mother/wife is either focussed elsewhere, or she no longer wants her husband but feels obliged to either remain in the marriage or feels unable to leave. This dynamic is quite often found in religious communities where couples have married young and are forced to remain together out of loyalty to a tradition, culture or religion, especially when the religion suppresses the sexuality of its female members. This however, mostly takes place at levels that are not fully conscious, but when a mother is confronted with such evidence through a constellation, her subconscious action (or lack thereof) becomes conscious and crystal clear. In my experience, every mother who has claimed 'not to have known' was not telling the truth. However, as Family Constellation work reveals truth in ways that are inescapable and undeniable, many women dealing with such incidents have been able to own their part. Having said this, it does not let the father off the hook, for each of us, irrespective of our reasons and impulses, are responsible for our own actions and the consequences of them. When such dynamics are revealed through Family Constellation work, it is the job of both parents to carry the burden of guilt and the consequences of their actions. This in turn totally frees the child to live and love in innocence once more. With this fresh approach to incest and sexual abuse, we are able to utilise the most simple and powerful forces known to humanity…the power of love. Through recognition of love, the child is redeemed and restored to her former state of innocence. The worst thing we could ever ask a child to do, is to take the stand and testify against her own father. It is as if her Soul will not allow her to do it—betray the very man who gave her life—and therefore call into question the value of her own life.

On hearing of this approach many individuals have strong objections to this work, feeling angered that the guilty are not punished or deemed less than worthy.

I was horrified and very angry when I heard you ask the client to say to the representative for her brother, "I allowed it out of love." I could never imagine feeling anything but hatred towards my father. But when I witnessed the silent and deeply touching moment when they embraced and she said, "You are still my brother, no matter what," I was moved to tears. I knew that this was what I needed to say in order to free myself from all the guilt I've been carrying. "Yes, (in tears) I love my father very much, and I miss him."

It is quite common that women who have been sexually abused as young girls find it very difficult to fully accept a husband. The underlying principle is that a girl who cannot fully accept her father as her father, will have great difficulty in fully accepting her husband, with all the consequences of relationship that follow. However, on being guided to the place of innocence that Family Constellation process can provide, she can once more fully accept her father as her father, and any man with whom she enters into relationship. For many, this is a difficult process, as there is a general feeling that those fathers who commit incest with their children, lose their rights as a parent. However, it must be stressed that this process is for the benefit of the child and in no way absolves either parent from their responsibility or guilt. An overriding principle is that when we deny the origins of our life, we will also deny ourselves in one way or another. An appropriate healing sentence might be, "No matter what happened, you remain my father and I remain your daughter."

Adoption

For the most part, couples who adopt children do so for their own reasons and not for the reasons of the child. Additionally, many adoptive parents do not give the honour and respect that is due to the biological parents and this has a negative impact on the adopted child. When children have been adopted owing to the unsupportive life conditions of the biological parents, be that drug addiction, alcoholism, illness, poverty or prostitution, many adoptive parents see themselves not only as the saviours of the child, but also as superior to their adoptive child's parents. Through Family Constellation work we have seen the importance of the connection to our parents and ancestors, and when an adoptive child's parents are not honoured, they lack a connection that can be a source of strength for them.

A few years back, I worked with an American couple who had an adopted son originating from Vietnam. They had decided to look at their child's problems in the context of Family Constellations as he was having difficulty with his studies and had drug and alcohol problems. My first question was to establish whether their son had access to Vietnamese culture in terms of food, language or contact with distant relatives. The answer I received was both shocking and very sad: "No, that country has nothing to offer him!" To deny a child's heritage—irrespective of how we may perceive either his parents or his country of origin—is to deny the child's right to be himself. Additionally, when entering the Knowing Field, it is clear that an adoptive child always belongs to his or her biological family, and sometimes, although rarely, to both the biological and adoptive families. What Vietnam had thereby offered this child was life itself and had offered the adoptive parents a precious gift. Vietnam had given much and had much more to offer their son.

When a child is offered up for adoption, it is almost as if a part of the child is killed; something is lost in the process. Our mother is the origin of love: she carries us in her body, she nurtures us, provides us with sustenance through breastfeeding...she is, in essence, our first experience of love and intimacy, and as children we have permission to enter those intimate spaces. When a child is denied that experience through being adopted, no matter how much the adoptive parents may love their new child, intimacy has died, making it difficult for adopted children to find their place, not only within themselves, but also in the world and with others. It is only when adoptive parents are able to fully honour the biological parents for the great gift that has been bestowed on them, that hope for the child survives.

In working with individuals who have been adopted, it has often been observed that they hold onto the dream that one day their mother will return, which can then lead them to seek their mother, or father, through other relationships. Whilst it is important for adopted children to feel connected to their roots and culture of origin, it is also important for them to release this dream so that they can live life to the fullest.

When a mother gives up a child for adoption—whether voluntarily or under duress from other family members—it has been observed that she often feels suicidal on some level, for the burden of guilt is too great for her to shoulder. If this mother then goes on to have other children and keeps them, often her other children—whether or not they are aware of their adopted sibling—feel a similar sense of guilt, or simply sense that something is missing in their lives, even to the extent of representing the adopted sibling in the family through taking on the adopted child's feelings of abandonment or through sabotaging their lives in order to share in the suffering of their sibling.

I've never given much thought to my adopted brother. My mother was very young, just a teenager at the time, and her parents encouraged her to give him up for adoption. When I entered the constellation and looked at the representative for my adopted brother, I was overwhelmed with emotion. It answered many of my questions about my feelings of sadness and that something was missing. Although I have never met him, I realise now that I miss him deeply. When I said the words, "Dear brother, it is such a pity that you had to leave because I've missed you deeply" it was if everything fell into place and on saying, "I take you fully as my brother and give you a place in my heart" I felt complete because that which was missing has now been found.

Abortion

When an abortion takes place as a result of medical reasons, the effects within the family are similar to those of a child who has died at an early age if this child is not given its proper place. However, when an abortion takes place purely for social reasons, the effects can be far-reaching.

My son is out of control. He's aggressive and violent towards me; I've even had to have a restraining order placed on him. His father and I are divorced, but nothing has happened in the family to cause this behaviour.

The above statement was made by a woman who attended a workshop looking for solutions to her relationship with her aggressive son. I asked her privately if she had had an abortion so as not to influence the representatives in her constellation. Without stating it out loud or informing the chosen representative, I placed a representative for the aborted child into the constellation so I could observe what the Knowing Field would tell us. As the aborted child was placed, the representative for her son clenched his fists and teeth, simply glaring at his mother and shouted, "You murderer!" Although this case is extreme, and I have only witnessed this particular scenario once, it serves to illustrate that the siblings of aborted children do feel it on some level, irrespective of whether the child was aborted prior to or after their own birth. From Family Constellation work, the Knowing Field clearly reveals that siblings are all aware of one another, whether or not they are actually born.

In working with many women who have had abortions for social reasons, I am yet to find a woman who does not either punish or sabotage herself in one way or another. The maternal instinct is so powerful, and the bonds of love between mother and child so strong, it simply seems to go against the grain to abort a child and this has often been observed as guilt carried by the Soul of the woman. When couples abort children they generally separate after a while. In a sense, the guilt of the couple urges them to sacrifice their love as a way of paying an unspoken form of penance. In many cases, when a woman decides to abort a child, she is saying to the man, "I want no part of you." The greatest impact of an abortion upon the mother and the family system is when the father is not informed, or when his request for the child to live is denied.

Miscarriages

When miscarriages take place, many different effects have been observed through working with the Knowing Field. The effects differ from family to family and couple to couple and much of it seems to depend on how long the pregnancy lasted and when the miscarriage took place. It is important to add, that many couples refer to children lost during the sixth month of pregnancy as a miscarriage, when in essence, it is either a stillborn child or a child who died shortly after birth. When such premature births are referred to as miscarriages, it is often done so in order to protect the parents from the grief of having lost a child. In this way, the child becomes forgotten and ousted from the family. From a family system perspective, again that which is excluded will be included and represented by another.

When the first pregnancy of a couple is miscarried, it can have a lasting effect not only on the parents, but also on the children who follow. In essence, the first pregnancy of a couple in love is the consummation of that love and the beginnings of their dreams of family. When this is shattered, the dream often begins to disintegrate and something is lost within the relationship, sometimes leading to separation. For the children who follow, the burden of this shattered dream can be great. Having lost their first child, the parents often find it difficult to fully bond with the following children, being afraid at some level that they may lose this child as well. Additionally, if the parents are unable to mourn for their child, and acknowledge the miscarriage as a child, then the following children can sense that something is missing, in the same or similar way to having a living sibling who died at an early age.

From an energetic point of view, it would seem that all children who are born are aware at different levels of all previous inhabitants of the mother's womb. Biologically we now know that stem cells can be harvested from any woman who has ever been pregnant, further testimony to the biological and energetic signature left behind by all pregnancies.

Trans-Generational Impact of Common Events

In traditional forms of therapy, common events are dealt with in the context of the present family, or the family of origin. However, for most us, we can get caught up in stories that we need to create in order to explain certain feelings and behaviour patterns that are disruptive in nature. As a means to explain feelings that they are unable to place logically into their lives, some also investigate the concept of past lives and karma. Although generally a believer in the eternal validity of the Soul and in re-incarnation, through observation and experience within the Knowing Field and Family Constellations, I am yet to find anything that suggests that we inherit feelings brought forward from past lives, but rather, answers to every problem a client has brought to me to work with can be found within the family, often stemming from events that took place three or more generations before.

The family Soul spans many generations and is comprised of the consciousness and conscience of each biological member of a family, with some notable exceptions.

The nature of the Soul is to be inclusive and we observe that that which is excluded on the human level, will be included on the level of the family Soul. Let us now discuss some of the exceptions.

Father's or Mother's First Love

On working with the Knowing Field through Family Constellations, events are often brought to light in terms of the impact which is not acknowledged as an issue by the client, but is evident, showing the results and impact on the family. More common than most would suspect, the first love of either mother or father can have a notable effect on children who are born to another partner. As stated many times, that which is excluded, or in this case, longed for, will be included by the family Soul. The Soul has an inner statement of inclusiveness and being equal to; a residual impact can be felt as a result of any relationship that is not ended with mutual love and respect. The following are some circumstances under which a first love relationship is ended that are often observed to have an impact on the new family:

• An individual falls in love with another, but owing to the demands of their culture, marries according to family custom and enters an arranged marriage.

Family Soul

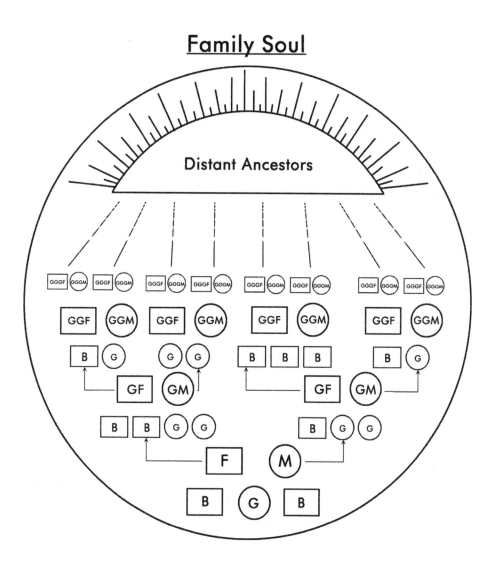

GGGF: Greatgreat Grandfather   GGF: Great Grandfather
GGGM: Greatgreat Grandmother   GGM: Great Grandmother
GF: Grandfather   GM: Grandmother   F: Father   M: Mother
B: Child - Boy G: Child - Girl

- A young couple is forced to separate as a result of pressure from family members owing to social, religious, ethnic or racial issues.

- One of the pair dies young as a result of an accident, war, illness or suicide.

- The relationship ends suddenly.

There is a poignant Dutch expression that sums up human response to first love: 'Eerste liefde roest niet' which means, 'First love never tarnishes'. Our first experience of intimacy, bonding and love is with our mother, and our first love represents our first reaching out for the experience of intimacy beyond our mother's sphere of influence. Therefore this experience creates a roadmap for life outside our family home and leaves a lasting impression.

When heterosexual couples fall in love and there is thought of marriage, there is generally a vision or a dream of starting a family and passing life on to their descendents. What we often see in Family Constellation work is that even though the relationship may have ended for some of the reasons stated above, the dream remains alive. In such cases, when a new relationship forms and children are born out of that, individuals can look upon their children as if they are the dreamt of children belonging to their first love. Given the examples above, it is to be noted that when a relationship is not concluded with mutual love and respect, honouring what was, then just as within a biological family, those who are excluded will be included through representation. The same can often be true for the first love...they become part of the family system. When this happens, the children of the new couple can become identified with their mother's or father's first love, which in turn creates confusion in terms of their identity. This can also lead them to take on the fate of one of their bereaved parents, or the fate of the first love.

This subconscious but powerful identification can lead to many disruptive life patterns for the children who follow. For example, a daughter who is identified with her mother's first love can find herself on a lifelong quest for the perfect man, in essence, living out her mother's loss of her great love. The same can also be true for young men who are identified with their father's first love. In such cases we often see that there is rivalry or disharmonious relationship between the children as there is a feeling of divided loyalties. One or more children can look to the father's first love as their mother, therefore becoming alienated from their own mother, or hold something against their father, which is not specifically known, out of loyalty to their mother. In some cases, it has been clearly seen that a young man, if identified with his father's first love, can represent her in the family through becoming feminised and homosexual. Another example of this I have observed, is that when a daughter becomes identified with her father's first love, it can lead to inappropriate sexual energies flowing between father and daughter, or even incest. One of the more common observances is that of a young woman who becomes 'daddy's little princess' where the daughter so strongly represents father's first love that she desires to take her mother's place at her father's side. Additionally, this type of entanglement can lead to alienation of the child representing the first love by one or both parents, as the child then represents that which doesn't want to be seen.

Often it is difficult for clients to conceive of such entanglements and identification with individuals they know little or nothing about and have probably never met. However, science, quantum physics and metaphysics are increasingly revealing how we are all part of a greater consciousness and awareness and are participants in that greater reality. For example, scientific experiments have shown that, when critical mass is reached within a species in terms of acquiring a new skill, all other members of that species will simply adapt the new behaviour instinctively. Similarly, we are not separate from our parents, in essence, we are them. Not only does our physical body result from their biology, but also our thought processes, feelings and attitudes develop from the blueprint that has been provided by them. It is interesting to note that with the advent of greater access to adoption records and biological parents in recent years, it has been found that many adopted children display behaviour and characteristic patterns that are close to or identical to their biological parents. Again, testimony to the unseen presence of the energy field of consciousness we have come to know as the Knowing Field within Family Constellation work. Although having said that, it is often difficult for clients to conceive of such identifications when the story is revealed through the Knowing Field; they invariably and undeniably experience it as true, as the feelings bubble up to the surface. No doubt, many of you reading these pages have already had feelings arising out of the examples given in this book, and it is through the awareness of such feelings that what was subconscious moves into the more conscious realm.

Murder and Unjust Death

Some years ago a client attended a workshop with the aim of gaining clarity in his life. He reported that people often did not trust him and were at times even afraid of him, being repulsed in some way. On investigating the facts of the family, it transpired that his grandmother had had an extra-marital affair with a local doctor. The doctor was involved in experimental treatments and drugs that were said to have improved health, none of which were part of an official study or development program; he was simply experimenting for his own purposes. As the relationship developed, the grandmother allowed the doctor to use experimental drugs on her infant child, the result of which was the death of the child. What was clear from the Knowing Field via the representatives was that neither grandmother nor the doctor could neither look at nor accept the consequences of their actions. In essence, the crime that was committed was denied. Through denied responsibility, the doctor, too, became part of the family system, and along with the dead child, the guilt of the grandmother, became represented in the family. The client in this instance was representing the doctor within the family and the reasons for other people's aversion to him became very clear. What is important to stress here, is that working with the Knowing Field not only reveals such entanglements, but also provides resolution through the use of healing sentences as previously discussed. During this family constellation, the client reported that he had indeed felt a sense of guilt and remorse all of his life but could not place it. The healing sentence he was guided to use was, "Dear Grandmother, I respectfully leave the guilt with you."

Another client, a young Jewish man, was aggressive, suffered from depression, and had violent tendencies. There was nothing specific from his childhood that would indicate a cause for such behaviour. However, it transpired that a great portion of his family had died during the Holocaust, and in one particular concentration camp. On asking him further details, he knew much about the camp commandant, his name, rank and family history. When the constellation was set up, it was noteworthy to witness that the young man's representative could not look at his family, but was transfixed by the representative for the camp commandant. Their body language, stance and attitude made it seem as if they were one and the same person. What eventually unfolded, was that he found it difficult, if not impossible, to look at those who had died and suffered in the camps, believing them to be weak in some way. Under such circumstances, the only place he could look was towards the perpetrator and represented him in his own life.

Ill-Gotten Gain

Some of the more notable examples of the impact of ill-gotten gain I have observed have been while working with Caucasian individuals in the state of Georgia in the USA. One particular middle-aged woman attended the workshop wanting to understand why her family was so 'cursed'. Again, within the context of Family Constellations, we focus much more on events, rather than on feelings. She reported that within her family there was a high level of both alcoholism and suicide, which seemed to have been going on for quite some time. She said that siblings, uncles, aunts, cousins and many individuals within her extended family had met this fate or had very disruptive lives. On investigation, it was revealed that her great-great-grandfather was a plantation owner. The land was originally the tribal land of a Native American nation that was removed with force, many of them dying in the process. Later, African slaves whom her great-grandfather had purchased worked the land. We set up the constellation to include her great-grandfather, representatives for the Native Americans, the slaves, and for those relatives who had either committed suicide or were alcoholic. The energy in the room was very intense and each of the representatives for her family members fell to the ground, crippled with both grief and inconsolable feelings of guilt and anguish. The family had been very wealthy, owning much land, and down through the generations much of it was lost through alcoholism, gambling and suicide. In order to bring balance and to pay a sort of penance for the wealth that was ill-gotten, family members were compelled to rid themselves of both their wealth and all of the blessings that life has to offer. In such cases, the freeing movement is one of honouring the fate of both the slaves and the Native Americans, giving each a place in their hearts and leaving the guilt with the grandfather.

One may wonder how something that seems very much like a role-play could become effective in changing such long-term familial destructive patterns. As we engage the Knowing Field, which connects us all to our ancestors and others who belong to the family system, not only does it inform us where the problems exist, but it also gives us an opportunity to change the influence of the field through silent body movement and the use of healing sentences. In a manner that one could compare to shamanistic ritual, it is as if an e-mail with the new information and solution is sent to the Souls of our ancestors who were involved, thereby bringing effective healing to the entire family system.

CHAPTER TWO

ILLNESS

Family Constellations as a Healing Process

Family Constellations as a healing modality contains different elements such as psychotherapeutic process, soul work, and ancestral work. With traditional psychotherapy, healing takes place over time and the therapist takes a very active role in directing the process, guiding his or her client to find strength from within. Additionally, traditional psychotherapy takes little or no account of the potential trans-generational aspects of the client's presented issue. On the other hand, in Family Constellations—while containing elements of psychotherapeutic process—the therapist is guided by the Knowing Field in order to find solutions. In this way, the facilitator of a Family Constellation process balances the dual role of therapist and healer: partially directing the healing process so that a resolution can be found, and in the role of a healer who simply holds the space for a solution to emerge. Furthermore, external elements such as connection to parents and ancestors are employed in order to assist the client in finding strength. In contrast to traditional psychotherapy, within the context of Family Constellation work we enter into the realm of the Soul. Through ancestral and Soul work, we work beyond the scope of the individual and enter into a healing process that can touch many generations of one or more families, and indeed communities. As the nature of the Soul lies beyond time, in many aspects, so does Family Constellation work. Within the process, lost children can be embraced once more, ex-lovers can be met and resolution found, and future possibilities can be met. Whereas psychotherapeutic process is linear in nature, constellation process is a moment in time that has no linear context. In other words, we work with the events and people of the past in order to effect healing in the present moment. The majority of participants experience immediate changes in real-time as opposed to a process that gradually unfolds. The effect of a family constellation is to create a new picture for the client, who can then take that new image into his or her Soul.

If we look at Family Constellation work as a combination of psychotherapeutic process and energy work, we can also see a direct correlation between this work and Brennan Healing Science. Brennan Healing Science is based on working directly with the human energy field and energy vortexes known as chakras, which are focussed along different points on the spine. This science has revealed that relationship cords connect us not only to our parents and siblings, but also to each and every intimate partner we have ever had, as well as to our ancestors. Having worked with several practitioners of this healing science over the past few years, the parallels between aspects of the two healing methods have become evident. Using Brennan Healing Science, the practitioner is able to restructure chakras and the relationship cords that emanate from them, connecting to other individuals. What has been observed is that unhealthy cords can exist between individuals and their ancestors, leading to the same dynamic that has been observed through family constellation work, namely, the individual carries the feelings of another and lives them as if they are her own. Family Constellation work together with Brennan Healing Science is paving the way towards a whole new concept of healing, a concept which says that we are much more than simply individuals...we are born into families, tribes and nations and these other groups we belong to can have a direct impact on our emotional, psychological and physical well being.

In addition to working directly on known issues such as intimate relationships and family matters, we are able to represent archetypes, concepts and entities within the Knowing Field. For example, nations, cultural elements such as religion, political movements and groups, plus the 'unknown' can enter into a constellation. Very often as a facilitator, I am able to bring in representatives for people or aspects that are unknown to the client or representative. Mostly this occurs as a result of a hunch, or simply because the representatives feel that someone or something is missing. What is remarkable about the Knowing Field, is that the significance of such a representative is almost instantaneously revealed. Often, after having placed such an unknown representative, a client will suddenly remember a piece of vital information such as, "I've just remembered that my great-grandmother had a stillborn child." In this way, the unseen intelligence of the Knowing Field informs us of events that are important. Let me give you an example.

In working with a client who was the child of immigrants, as I rounded off a constellation, I added a representative for her parents' country of origin,

Portugal, in order to strengthen her sense of belonging and connection to her ancestors. However, as is my custom, I did not name this representative. However, to my surprise, none of the other representatives were particularly happy with the placement which puzzled me. Assuming that some other problem stemming from the homeland had been revealed, I asked my client what had happened in Portugal. She could not identify anything specifically. I then revealed to the client that the representative was 'Portugal' to which she replied, "But I'm not Portuguese, we are from Madeira." On replacing Portugal for a representative for Madeira, all of the representatives smiled, stood strongly and chests puffed up with pride. My assumption regarding her heritage led to the revealing of the power of the Knowing Field and stood as testimony to the power of our connection to our ancestors. Although the island of Madeira belongs to Portugal, Madeirans consider themselves a separate Portuguese ethnic group.

Physical Illness and Disease

Many individuals attend Family Constellations owing to serious illness. Great value in constellation work has been evident in the results that have been achieved over the years. However, the purpose of working in this way with illness is not to work directly with the illness, having the objective of finding a cure as such, but it is to look at the family system to which the client belongs. We do have the choice of setting up a complete family constellation where the theme of the client is their illness. We also have the option of simply setting up a representative for the client and a representative for the named illness in order to see what transpires regarding the family system. When a client with a serious illness attends a workshop, we gather information about events in the family in the usual way in order to reveal and release the underlying tensions allowing the client to draw upon his own natural healing power.

What has been observed is that when individuals are drawn towards deceased members of the family, their life-force energy is weakened, leading to vulnerabilities in the body that can manifest as illness.

A client had been suffering from blinding headaches for several years. No neurological problem had been identified and the client had been taking large doses of pain killers for quite some time; however, his headaches were still debilitating and he frequently had to spend time in bed away from work. On setting up his constellation, the representative for his headache fell to his knees holding the top of his head as he did so. The client revealed that his parents had a son who was born a few years prior to him who had died in an accident. The cause of death was a rock that had fallen onto his head as a result of assumed negligence by another family member. The client's headaches disappeared on that day and have rarely recurred since.

In working this way, we are able to bring clients face to face with those who have died, so that a resolution can be found. If resolved, and the client is able to gain strength from this meeting, it will have a positive influence on his overall energy field, greatly improving the likelihood of recovery. What is important to remember in such cases, is that when parents are unable to look at a dead child—blocked by their own feelings of guilt—the child, in essence, becomes excluded from the family. The nature of both the individual Soul and the family Soul is to be inclusive of all things, and in this way, our client with the headaches included his brother by representing the earlier fatal accident through manifesting headaches.

In the healing process, such clients must first relinquish their unspoken loyalty to the one who has died in a tragic accident…this is often no small feat. Our entanglement with the fate of others often comes from a sense of 'it should never have happened' or 'someone must pay for this deed', the underlying feeling of the parents. A movement towards freedom from such entanglements is to submit to the fate of others. Through the Family Constellation process, we get to know that there are two kinds of entanglement in the family system. First there is fate, and second, the business of others. When entangled in the fate of others, we are rarely consciously aware of it; however, it does come into awareness during Family Constellations process. When we are entangled in the business of others, it is mostly conscious, for example, objection to the new husband our widowed mother has chosen. Most of our problems stem from being involved in those things that are beyond the realm of our personal control, and constitute the business of others.

Loyalty to parents and family

Very often we observe that serious illness seems to arise out of a strong sense of loyalty to one or more family members.

A client with breast cancer revealed that both her mother and grandmother had died relatively young as a result of breast cancer. As the family story was revealed, we discovered that my client's great-grandmother had died along with her young son in the British concentration camps of the Anglo-Boer War in South Africa, leaving her daughter behind, who was the client's grandmother. As we set up the constellation, the client both wept and smiled, she seemed happy to share a similar fate. After much inner work, she was able to bow to the fate of her great-grandmother and her son, and was also able to give a place in her heart to the British captors. On meeting her great-grandmother and her great-uncle, she could clearly see that their Souls were weakened by her wanting to die out of loyalty to them, and in contrast were strengthened when she bowed to their fate.

When clients attend workshops in order to investigate and work with serious illness, it is important to gain information about any other family member who has suffered from the same illness. When the same illness occurs amongst several family members, it can gain great power within the family, especially when the medical field supports the hold the illness has over the family by indicating a sealed fate in terms of genetic inheritance. More often than not, we can observe an entanglement in the fate of others and significant events taking place within a family when we work with generational illness and disease. When the story and the identification with others come to light, it is then that resolution becomes possible.

Suffering on Behalf of Others

Suffering on behalf of others is a common theme we see in Family Constellation work. Such suffering not only manifests as physical illness, but also as disruptive life patterns. When illness is observed within the context of an entanglement with one who has suffered, it is not necessarily an identical illness that manifests. Often, when individuals who are entangled with the fate of one who has died tragically, unlawfully, or has been forgotten, it is the drain on their physical organism that leads to the development of illness and disease. When we are identified with one who has died, we have one foot in the grave so to speak, and therefore we are not fully present in physical life. From an energetic perspective, there are cords of energy that connect us primarily from the first chakra to our biological family and ancestors. This energy centre at the base of the spine, often referred to as the base chakra, represents our will to live in the physical body and our sense of being present in life on earth. However, relationship cords can, and indeed do, have an impact on our physical well being as has been demonstrated many times within this healing process. The first chakra—directly related to our physical apparatus—when damaged or drained by unhealthy relationship cords to ancestors, a parent or grandparent, can weaken the overall health of the physical body and have an impact on the immune system; this can lead to the development of various cancers, AIDS and other immune system related illnesses. When looking at illness, we can almost always assume that it is either directly or indirectly a result of damaged relationship cords and possible entanglement within the family system.

Damage to the base chakra is traditionally seen as being caused by early childhood trauma or a birth trauma that disrupts a child's ability to connect fully to the physical body and physical environment, or to one or both parents. Such trauma can cause an individual to withdraw from physical life—never making a full connection to the physical world or the body—and can lead to a lack of nurturing for the body in terms of 'chi', or universal energy. Other experiences, such as the early death of a parent, abandonment or divorce can also lead to damage in the base chakra energy system. However, through Family Constellation work, we have observed that the trauma may indeed belong to someone else in the family system and the effects of this trauma can become manifest within an individual as if the person had experienced it firsthand, even though there is no conscious awareness of the problem. Relationship cords that connect us to ancestors who are part of an unhealed trauma from the past can drain our physical system in the same way that direct experience of a trauma can. In essence, the broad spectrum of healing has opened up beyond the individual to the family and it has become apparent that individuals cannot heal themselves as if they were an island, but only as one part of a family system. In a similar way, a directly experienced trauma can create a drain on our physical body and health, and it is true that the trauma experienced by a brother, a beloved aunt or any other family member, can manifest itself within us as if it were our own.

A woman in her late thirties was emaciated through years of struggle with anorexia and bulimia. On investigating her family system through constellation work, the story of her mother's family came to light. Several members of her mother's family had starved to death in the Netherlands during the Second World War. As the war was never spoken about and these relatives never mentioned, they had in effect, become forgotten…their fate never accepted. My client was deeply entangled with the fate of those who had starved to death and felt compelled to represent them in this way.

However, it has also been seen that the entanglement does not always have to be with a direct family member but could be with one who is associated with the family in some way.

Gudrun, although having three children, was suffering a relapse of bulimia after many years of struggling with her illness in her teens and twenties. She was in physical crisis and her medical practitioners were warning her of possible complications with her heart and other major organs owing to malnutrition. Gudrun was just a little more than skin and bone when we met. On investigating her family history I learned that her grandfather had been a Nazi officer in Auschwitz and had little or no remorse for his actions in those days. The war was never discussed in Gudrun's family and the details of her grandfather's activities had been a long-standing family secret. On setting up her constellation, we placed her grandfather and several representatives for his victims in Auschwitz. What was clear from the outset was that Gudrun wanted to stand alongside the emaciated victims of the Holocaust as a representative for that which was a secret within her family. Gudrun later revealed her deep interest in Kaballah and other Jewish traditions, claiming that she had once considered converting to Judaism.

In the case of Gudrun, she was not suffering on behalf of a family member, but on behalf of the victims of her grandfather who had been forgotten and denied. Time and again, we are reminded through Family Constellation work, that nothing is ever truly forgotten or excluded; another will simply champion their cause, usually unconsciously, compelled by an inner impulse, however irrational it may seem. The Soul is inclusive of all things, and that which is excluded or denied will be represented as the result of the Soul's compulsion to include through representation. In this way, Family Constellation work bridges the gap between psychotherapy and Soul work, for in essence, not only do we work with the living through representation, we also work with the dead. Clients often ask me if the Souls of those who have already died gain healing from the work that we have done in a workshop. My response has always been, "I don't really know, I only concern myself with the benefits gained by the living." One day a client called me enthusiastically on the phone, wanting to relate an important story. She had attended family constellations two or three times and we had done some work that had involved her deceased grandmother. Julia, my client, explained to me that every year for the past several years she had visited a spirit medium on or around her birthday in order to gain spiritual insights for the year to come. On this occasion, her grandmother had spoken through the medium and thanked her for the healing work that had taken place and said that she was feeling much better. Neither the medium nor Julia had discussed family constellation work during the session prior to the grandmother's communication. When such stories are shared, we need to look at them at face value and not add conjecture or create other stories in support of them, but simply accept what has been said without drawing further conclusions. In this way we protect the integrity of the effectiveness of healing work done on behalf of the client, and avoid sensationalising that which ultimately cannot be proven. However, I have heard a number of stories similar to this one.

Sarah was a young woman in her late twenties who suffered from uncontrollable crying. She explained that she started crying in her mid-teens and that now her life felt totally controlled by it. She cried almost all the time and felt it was difficult to make friends, have intimate relationships or even be out in public. Much therapy of different varieties had never been able to reveal the source of her constantly flowing tears. On investigating her family history, Sarah revealed that she was part American Indian on her mother's side, but that her mother had forbidden her to tell anyone as she feared discrimination in the southern U.S. state in which she lived. On telling the story of her family, Sarah revealed that her full-blooded Native American great-grandmother, who had been kept a secret for so long, had been forcibly removed by the authorities from the state of Georgia along with her people, in order to be settled in a reservation. This mass forced migration of Native Americans was aptly called 'The Trail of Tears'.

Schizophrenia

Stephan was a young man in his early thirties who originally attended Family Constellation work because he was having problems within his marriage. He revealed that he had been diagnosed as having a light form of schizophrenia. Some other clients who had attended workshops when Stephan was present expressed their discomfort with him as he had what seemed to be an aggressive and hostile nature, although it was never expressed. Certain people were simply afraid of him and Stephan was able to confirm that it was a problem for him at times. On asking Stephan about the form and nature of his schizophrenia, he shared that he could frequently hear a scream in his head, and the voice did not sound like his own. He also felt that his life had been cursed as many things simply went wrong.

On asking him about his family history, it was revealed that although he was German, his mother was a German Jew and most of her family had died in the Nazi concentration camps while his father's family had been Germans who were actively involved in WWII. He admittedly felt very split between being a German and being a Jew and had tried for some time to deny his Jewish heritage. When I asked him if there had been any specific events that he knew of in the family regarding the war or those who went to the concentrations camps, he shared a harrowing story about his great aunt. He explained that on the day before Hitler's birthday the camp commandant had come to his aunt and told her that as part of a celebration for Hitler's birthday, her young son would be cremated in the ovens without being gassed beforehand, in other words, burned alive. The commandant gave his aunt the choice of either killing her own son, or sending him to that horrible fate. His aunt chose to kill her own son in order to spare him the suffering.

When we set up the constellation, we chose representatives for Stephan, the camp commandant, Stephan's great aunt and her son. Immediately the representative for Stephan's great aunt reported, "It's the most terrible feeling I have ever felt, I feel a loud scream welling up inside of me, it's overpowering, it's terrible." Feeling that it was necessary, I encouraged his great aunt's representative to allow the scream to be voiced. It was the most spine-chilling sound I had ever heard. Stephan sobbed and said, "That's the sound in my head, that is what I often hear." Stephan was strongly identified with the camp commandant, and equally so with his great aunt, finding it difficult to choose between the two.

Over a period of several months, Stephan attended numerous Family Constellation workshops and his mental state began to improve. Additionally, as we worked on his identification with the camp commandant, his aggression began to soften, so much so, that the other clients who were originally afraid of him, began to grow in fondness for him. Stephan has since reported that he no longer hears the scream and attends synagogue occasionally with another friend who is also from a mixed family.

Bi-Polar

Paul was a 21-year-old gay man who had been diagnosed as bi-polar at the age of sixteen. He had felt suicidal for several years and had worked as an escort at a gay brothel for about a year. At the time of meeting, Paul, apart from his life partner, had no friends, no job, and spent up to fourteen hours a day in bed, only getting dressed to face his day minutes before his boyfriend returned home from work. In essence, he was not living. He had been in therapy for quite some time which had revealed that the source for his suicidal tendencies was his parent's divorce and his father's rejection of his homosexuality.

The first time I set up a constellation for Paul, I suspected something dire in his mother's family but could not put my finger on it; Paul was unable to confirm anything as he had little information about his mother's family. The second time he visited a workshop, my sense of something dire in his mother's family became stronger, it was very palpable. However, as Paul was so young and vulnerable, I chose to work on simpler aspects of his constellation. When he returned a third time I said to him, "I think there has been a murder in your family, do you know anything about it? It seems to have something to do with your grandmother." His response was at first shock, then anger. He was incensed that I could suggest such a thing.

A few days later, he called and reported that a very strange thing had happened. He had gone to visit his sick mother who spontaneously started to talk about her family. He reported that his mother had said, "There's a strange story about your great-grandmother. Her daughter died mysteriously and many in the family suspected that she had murdered her own child." This was sufficient to get Paul's attention and motivate him to return to Family Constellations once more. Now that we had the information, we could set up a constellation with representatives for his mother, grandmother, great-grandmother and the daughter who had died. What was clear from Paul's constellation, was that he was identified with the daughter who had died, to the extent that when the representative for this murdered child laid down as if dead, Paul was compelled to lay down next to her, as if dead himself. His life until that point certainly reflected that.

After a couple more constellations, Paul reported that under the guidance of his doctor he was off medication, was no longer sleeping more than seven hours a night, and was attending classes at a local vocational college.

Suicidal Tendencies

Therapy often approaches suicidal tendencies from the perspective of looking at life circumstances in order to pinpoint the originating cause. Typically, divorce in the family, difficulties at school or in the workplace, financial problems and low self-esteem, are usually identified as the root cause. However, Family Constellation work has revealed that something quite different is responsible.

The Orders of Love dictate that what has been forgotten or cast out will be represented by others in the family system. In every case of suicidal tendencies I have dealt with over the past few years, I have always found that the suicidal individual is either drawn directly to a family member who is already dead, or that he has taken on the suicidal feelings of other family members. The influence of the dead can span many generations and when their fate is either not accepted or denied, the influence of the dead can be detrimental rather than being a healthy support of ancestral energies. Whenever I deal with a suicidal client, or a client with suicidal tendencies, I first draw a genealogy map of the family, spanning as many generations as I can in order to identify possible problem areas. Commonly, when a parent lost his own mother or father at a young age, one of his children will take on the father's longing to be with his parent and will develop suicidal tendencies as a result of his identification with the dead. Similarly, from a broader trans-generational aspect, I have seen these tendencies arise amongst the children of parents who are descendants of ethnic groups who have lost many family members owing to persecution and war. The Holocaust, African slavery and the Pogroms are three examples of such trans-generational effects.

AIDS and HIV

Setting up constellations for AIDS and HIV sufferers have been heart-wrenching and deeply moving. Not from the perspective of any kind of special sympathy I feel for such individuals, but from the point of view of what the constellation story reveals. When individuals with AIDS and HIV set up their constellations, it is often very clear from the outset that there is a very strong will to die. More often than not, there is a deep family grief that is commonly hidden at first, but suddenly reveals itself in a fairly dramatic fashion as a story of intense trauma. As HIV and AIDS are diseases of the immune system, I have always found that such individuals are identified with someone who died young, tragically or unlawfully, and this identification is creating an energetic drain on the physical system. What I have seen with many gay men infected with these diseases is that they frequently offer themselves up as a sacrifice to the family system, being willing to die for the sake of their mother who carries an unbearable burden, or another female within the family system.

George, a gay man in his late thirties when I first worked with him, shared with me that his father had died when he was eleven years old. During his constellation he expressed in the cry of a traumatised child, "I just want to be with my daddy!"

One of the tragedies with AIDS and HIV amongst gay men is that as individuals, many of them have been rejected either outright, or in other ways, by one or both parents. On the surface it appears that the rejection has to do with their sexuality or their disease. However, from a systemic point of view, such individuals have become the family scapegoat as they are, more often than not, identified with either a family trauma or grief that is not acknowledged, or with an individual who has also been cast out. I have even seen cases where the gay man with AIDS is paying a kind of penance for an injustice that has taken place within the family—we are reminded of the biblical saying, "The sins of the father will be visited upon the son." Before anyone assumes that I've just stated that AIDS is a punishment, let me reiterate. Family systems only deal with internal psychological forces, not with external forces. Guilt drains the energy of a family Soul and some members are more susceptible than others, with some individuals taking on or embodying the entire burden of family guilt. This in itself drains the immune system.

Myalgic Encephalomyelitis (ME)/Chronic Fatigue Syndrome (CFS)

Susan was a healthy career woman until the symptoms of ME/CFS surfaced at the age of 34. When first working with her I asked, "Who had reason to be this tired in your family?" Susan was unsure. Her constellation revealed that her grandmother had lost four children between the ages of two and four from various illnesses. On asking the grandmother's representative how she felt, she replied, "I'm exhausted and can barely stand." Susan's identification with her grandmother was a result of feeling the need to support her grandmother as her grandfather had turned away from his wife emotionally after the death of the children. The burden of grief was simply too much to carry on her own, and so was shouldered by another family member, in this case, Susan. After her first constellation, Susan reported feeling more energised than she had in several years. We continued to work together and gradually she gained what she called a 'normal' life. However, this all took work on Susan's part, for she initially had resistance to leave to another that which belonged to them.

Beyond Illness

In the past few years working with Family Constellations, I have only had the privilege of working with one trans-sexual client on two separate occasions. My client, now female, was born male. What her constellation revealed very clearly was that in her family system there was a strong impulse towards violence through the male line. Men in the families of both parents had been noted military men and had been involved in the deaths of civilian populations. In order to resist the violent impulse coming through the male line, my client felt compelled to remove all signs of maleness from his body and submit to a sex change operation. In addition to resisting the male line, there was also an apparent identification with the civilian female victims of his ancestor's violence. In conclusion, we cannot approach setting up a constellation with the view of either 'healing' or 'fixing' a problem. It is very clear that for this client, no resolution could be found or felt until her difficult fate was acknowledged and accepted. The inner movement with this client was not to change what is, but simply to accept it, which in turn brings about inner peace.

CHAPTER THREE

ACKNOWLEDGING
AND ACCEPTING WHAT IS

The power of Family Constellation work derives not only from Healing Sentences and from the Knowing Field itself, but from the basic principles of acknowledging what is, devoid of pretences, stories and judgments we have created.

What is very clear as a result of much exposure to Family Constellation work, is that most, if not all, of our problems come from being involved either in the business or fate of another. When we look at a family system, it is often revealed that individuals are tied up in the fate of others, carrying their burdens and feelings as their own. For many, this is not clear to them until they experience their own family constellation. However, many are consciously entangled and resist letting go of their entanglement with others, be that out of loyalty, a sense of superiority, or an inner dialogue that says, "I can do it better" or "I am more capable than the other of carrying the burden."

In her book, *Loving What Is*, Byron Katie talks of three kinds of business: mine, yours and God's. Within the context of Family Constellations, we can substitute "God's Business" for fate.

I am reminded of a client I worked with some years ago whose father had been in a severe accident that had mentally and physically debilitated him, the result being that the father had spent more than twenty years in a care facility and no longer recognised members of his family. The client's mother was now dating a man and had plans to marry again and wished to divorce her disabled husband. However, two of the client's siblings stood in the way, and under duress, the mother ended her relationship with the new man. Although the loyalty of the children to the disabled father is understandable, this is a clear example of how they were entangled in their mother's business. Through Family Constellation work, individuals can come to a greater understanding of who belongs and who does not, thereby coming to know that their father will always be their father, their parents always their parents, irrespective of any future relationship that the mother may form. Through Family Constellations work, we as children, learn that what belongs to the parents must be left there, the result of which is greater peace and harmony in our own lives.

Getting Out of the "Story"

Many therapists will tell you that if they were to ask more than one sibling from the same family to describe their parents, childhood and family, the therapist could easily assume that each sibling was born to different parents. This happens not only owing to the differing life circumstances of the family though the passage of time, thereby giving each child a different image and set of memories according to their order of age, but also owing to individual perception. Each of us creates our own vision of reality as we grow up. Some of that vision is passed onto us by our parents through the stories they tell and the sharing of their beliefs about the world; however, much of the vision is created through our own free will to choose what we wish to focus on and make true for ourselves.

For example, one client described his father as being strict and unfeeling, whilst his brother described their father as an educator who wanted to encourage his children to get the most out of life's experiences. So which story is true? The answer is, both and neither. Neither story is provable with certainty, even by the individuals who hold the stories as true. The question that must be asked—if stories and perceptions are not provable—is what value do they have to offer us? While stories which make us feel good such as, "My father loved me" can benefit us in terms of our sense of self-esteem, they are not useful when coupled with the polarity of, "Father was good" and "Mother was bad," or vice versa, as we end up with split loyalties which create a burden.

In working with many hundreds of individuals it appears to me that, to some extent, all of us are tied up in stories that are not provable. For example, at the beginning of each workshop or private session, I clearly state what information is important to know prior to working with clients, in terms of who belongs to their family, specific events, deaths, miscarriages, divorces, etc. Despite this, the majority of clients, when asked to tell me about their family, start with something like this, "My mother was a jealous person and did not get on with our neighbours", "My father loved his work more than he loved us children" or "My sister was definitely the favourite child."

Our experience of reality and our perception of it are created by the stories we have made true for ourselves. When we create the story, "My father loved his work more than he loved me," that can easily translate in adult life to a belief that the men in your life love their work more than they love you, which is a perception, which in turn can create the experience of reality where you choose a partner who indeed does spend more time at work than with you. However, in and of itself, that does not mean that he loves his work more than you, for he may be operating from a different belief system. The father or husband who spends a lot of time at work could be operating from the belief that working long hours to ensure financial well being is an act of love for his family. In this way, all statements such as, "My father loved his work more than he loved me" cannot be proven, and yet, we choose to make this our story, and the filter through which we look at life.

Through the process of Family Constellation work, we strip the stories bare and simply look at the family system. In this arena that is devoid of stories and individual perceptions, the truth of the natural love between family members can be revealed. However, in order for a constellation to work, we must be willing to surrender our stories and face the deeper question: do we want peace, or do we want to be right?

Investigating the Truth

When we think of our families we tap into feelings that have been born out of the stories we have created. You may start with a statement like, "My mother didn't really want me, I'm sure of that, because she never showed me any affection." As we become older and wiser we may change that to, "My mother found it difficult to show me love." However, in most cases, the evolution of our story is not the complete truth, or simply denies a truth that does not fit in with our view on reality, what love is, and how it is expressed.

For example, a client felt wounded that her mother never showed her any love. I pointed out to her that she was blinded by placing conditions upon the unconditional love she was demanding. On giving her the example of how men often interpret showing love as working long hours to support their families, she began to ask herself from which paradigm of love her mother might be operating. During our earlier conversation, she complained that her mother was always 'fussing' over her, attending to things that she felt she, as the grown daughter, was more than capable of doing for herself, like tidying her room when she came to visit, doing her laundry, ironing clothes, etc. I offered her the suggestion that perhaps her mother believed that doing things for her children was the way to show love. The tension that had arisen between mother and daughter over the years came largely from the daughter's resistance to her mother's love. Several weeks later my client went to visit her mother for a weekend and simply allowed her mother to fuss over her, cook, do laundry, wait on her every need, and to do so without any need for her daughter's help with household chores. My client simply sat, did nothing and allowed her mother to do all that she did without resistance. She reported that even though she had some difficulty with her mother seemingly invading her space and doing everything for her, her mother actually touched and caressed her a couple of times that weekend, for the first time in many years. So what really happened here? The daughter ceased putting conditions on love, ceased resisting her mother's way of being and doing, and actually received her mother's love. Instead of the usual tension between them, the mother glowed, for she was finally free to express her love in her own way, and the daughter left the family home after that weekend with a special place in her heart for her mother. At a very deep level she realised that her story of her mother not really wanting her or loving her was not true at all and that she had wasted much time in holding her life hostage to this false story.

Many of us demand from our parents that they be superhuman, able to express and show their maximum capacity for love at all times. However, parents, like us, fall short of perfection, for they, too, belong to family systems where the flow of the Orders of Love has been interrupted. What many of us do is stubbornly refuse to accept the love that is present, preferring instead to place conditions upon unconditional love by saying, "This is how I want you to show me love and how often." Constellation work has shown us that when we submit fully to what is there, the flow of love between parents and children, partners, spouses and friendships will simply increase. Perhaps as a child you remember visiting your grandmother who used to make the most delicious cakes, puddings and biscuits for you. You loved her dearly and you remember her as kind, gentle and loving…all because she expressed her love through baking for her beloved grandchild. This kind of experience leaves a deep impression on a child and as you grow up, you may very well associate the baking, buying or giving of cakes, puddings and biscuits as an expression of love. It then follows that you may bake, buy and give such sweet delights to your friends for birthdays, when they're sick, holidays and at other times when you wish to say, "I love you." Now let's imagine that you visit a friend, who upon seeing your cake declares, "Thank you, but I'm on a diet." The general result is that you will feel wounded and rejected. It really isn't about the cake is it? No, you feel wounded because your love paradigm tells that you that your love has been rejected. Likewise, if your friend eats your cake and tells you how delicious it is, it still isn't about the cake. For you, your friend is telling you, "Your love is good enough" or "I acknowledge your love, and it is good."

Each of us has our own unique concept of love—what it is, and how to show and share it. When we turn our back on love because it doesn't come in the form that we want, demand or expect, we impoverish our own lives and stop the natural flow of love between ourselves and the other, and both parties end up feeling unacknowledged and wounded to a greater or lesser degree. If we look to another for love, and this other is only able to give and express fifteen percent of her total love, our job is to submit fully to the fifteen percent available to us. In this way, not only do we serve ourselves, but we also serve the other. For as we truly acknowledge in our heart what is there, we encourage the increased flow of love. After my client had submitted to her mother 'fussing' over her, almost overnight her perception changed to one of, "My mother really does love me a lot" and in doing so, part of the affection she was looking for, came her way in small doses that gradually increased with each visit. Her mother felt elated that her love was finally being acknowledged and received, and the daughter felt like a child again as she allowed her mother to dote on her. The moral of this story is that if we want *anything* to change, we must first change our perception, thinking, expectations and attitude. As the daughter changed these things, her mother changed, too. But did the mother really change? No. The daughter simply opened to what was already there. It was only her resistance and perception that had deemed it to be insufficient.

Self-Deception and the Perpetuation of Falsehood

Many of us have stories of how we weren't loved, how we were disrespected, abused and hurt by others, be that at the hands of other family members or of former partners. Just as our stories form the basis of our perception of reality, the stories themselves create the way in which we interact with our reality and the people in it. Additionally, they form our expectations of what we feel we are able to receive in life or are worthy of receiving.

On working with a client who had experienced an incestuous sexual relationship with her brother four years her senior, it was clear that she had a strong perception of herself as an abused victim. The story was taboo within her family and as a result, she felt deeply shamed. In cases of incest, moral judgments about sexuality—especially incest—disallow victims of incest to love their abusers. This is not only discouraged by other family members, but also by churches and, sadly, by many therapists. On working directly with her, I asked how she felt about her brother. She replied, "I hate him, he ruined my life." I then asked, if she had the permission of her parents to love her brother, how would she feel about him? She broke down in tears and uttered through her sobs, "I love my brother so very much and I miss him." During a constellation I had her say to a representative for her brother, "I allowed it out of love for you, and that love was innocent." She sobbed once more, turned to me and said, "It feels like the whole world has lifted off my shoulders." I told her that it was because she felt innocent once more.

What she learnt from this very simple exercise was that she was the perpetrator of continuing abuse against herself, for as she denied her love for her brother, she denied herself love and denied love to the men in her life, especially her husband. Likewise, whether the sexual abuser was a father, a mother, an uncle or a family friend, when a client is able to say, "I allowed it out of love for you," she is released from the guilt and regains her innocence once more. This way of working is difficult for some to accept at first, as society has taught us that the guilty must be punished and that we do so by withdrawing our love from them, not by acknowledging the love that is there.

For an individual who has been sexually abused by a parent, her place in life can become virtually untenable. For example, if the father, the one who initiates life, is the abuser, then the child is often forced to deny the love that she will naturally have for the one who gave the gift of life. When we ask victims of incest to withdraw their love from a parent, not only do they remain 'guilty', but they also deny themselves life. With the many wounded individuals I have worked with who have experienced incest with a parent, almost without exception, they have been able to feel the deeper truth in the healing sentence, "I allowed it out of love for you." What leaves some observers of this work unsatisfied is the need for the father (or mother) to be vilified and punished in some way, as if the acknowledgement of this innocent love somehow absolves the perpetrator of wrongdoing. The acknowledgement of the innocent love of the child releases the child and frees her to love the parent as a parent; the perpetrator is left with the burden of guilt and the child is finally free. Our need to punish the guilty simply keeps their victims imprisoned in shared guilt and shame. As love is acknowledged, the victim no longer needs to carry that guilt and shame and respectfully returns it to where it belongs.

Likewise, in matters of divorce and separation from an intimate partner, many of us perpetuate stories that can keep us hostage, and when children are involved, can shame our children. For example, a divorced woman came to work with me as she was having difficulties with her relationship with her son. My first question was about the father and her instant change in body language and demeanour made it clear that she had anger towards him. On observing this I said to her, "Your son is angry with you because you don't respect his father." "How could I," she retorted. "He was unfaithful and left me for the other woman." On further investigation, it turned out that her mother had died when she was only sixteen and she had become best friends with her father…in a sense replacing her own mother. On this realisation, she gained the insight that she had never really been available to her husband, for she had been 'married' for many years to her father. During the constellation I had her say to a representative for her husband, "I am deeply sorry I was not available to you, I was too busy with my father." On saying these words, the love between the couple was clear to see, for both she and her husband's representative had moved back to the time when they fell in love. At this point, she turned to the representative for her son and said, "I honour the part of your father I see alive in you, and it is good to see." The son immediately relaxed and felt moved to embrace both of his parents. At the end of the constellation, I gently told my client that at times, infidelity is the solution, not the problem. She smiled, then sobbed a little and said, "Yes, I've been creating a lot of difficulties for myself and my son, I can see that now." What is important to remember when it comes to divorce and separation, especially when children are involved, is that there was a time when we loved our partner and the only reason anger, bitterness and hurt exist within us is because our love for them continues. In general, the deeper the negative emotion towards a former partner, the deeper the love that existed between them. When we can acknowledge that love and leave it with peace, we are free to truly love again. Until that time, no matter whom we marry or with whom we enter into a relationship, we will remain with one foot in the former marriage or partnership. It is said that 'The truth shall set you free'. In my observation, truth is almost always about love, in one form or another—distorted or otherwise—and it is love that has been uncomplicated by the story that sets us free.

Releasing Resistance

Most of us have quite clear ideas about what we want in life. We want a satisfying job, fruitful relationships, loving partnerships, good health and financial security. However, in working with people I have noticed that most of us spend most of our time resisting the things that we don't want, or simply focusing on what we don't like. Let me give you an example.

A married man in his mid-thirties attended a workshop as he was having some difficulties in his relationship with his wife. When I asked what he wanted out of the relationship he answered, "I want to stop arguing with my wife and I want her to be less jealous." Is it clear to you that he didn't answer my question? I did *not* ask him what he *didn't* want; I asked what he *did* want. There is a great difference between the two. When we think we are stating what we want, but focus on what we don't want, our energies and attention are drawn to those situations. As our attention is drawn there, our focus simply collects more evidence from our lives that it is full of what we don't want.

However, resistance goes much deeper than simply getting clear about what we *do* want. Earlier we spoke about three kinds of business: our business, the business of others, and fate. Most of our resistance and suffering comes from resisting conditions and business that is not even ours. For example, we could bemoan the financial policies of our government and spend much of our time complaining about the economy. However, in reality, the force that put the government into place is far greater than us; it falls into the realm of fate. Perhaps millions of individuals voted for the particular government in question and that, in itself, places it in the realm of fate. There's nothing you can do to change the situation until the next opportunity to vote, and even then nothing may change. In these kinds of situations, we have the choice of *choosing* what we want to create in our life or focus on what cannot be changed, thereby shifting our energies onto that which is not wanted.

Another level of resistance is resisting who we are in terms of our heritage. For example, a client of mine who was half Dutch and half Afro-Caribbean preferred to think of himself as Afro-Caribbean as he felt ashamed of the role of the Dutch in African slavery. He initially attended a Family Constellations workshop, as his life was basically not working. His finances were insufficient, his health was poor and his intimate relationships were virtually non-existent. He sincerely felt that he was doing everything right and couldn't understand why nothing seemed to be going the way he wanted. After hearing his story, I looked at the client and said, "How could you expect your life to work for you when you deny those who gave you life?" He was quite startled by my question and replied, "Oh no, you don't understand. I don't have any issues with my parents." To which I replied, "But you do with your Dutch ancestors." I went on to explain that through denying his Dutch ancestors, he denied his own life, and the life of his mother and all of his Afro-Caribbean relatives and ancestors. He looked quizzical. I explained that the fate of the African slaves had created his life and that in fact, without slavery he simply wouldn't exist. He looked at me intensely when I suggested that he bow before a representative for the Dutch slave masters who had brought his mother's ancestors to the Caribbean. His intense look was one of outrage. I then reminded him of the three kinds of business: his, other people's, and fate. I asked him directly, "Are you bigger than the power of fate?" "No," he replied. I asked, "Who are you to dictate what should or should not have happened so many generations ago? You are simply making yourself bigger and more important than you are." His tone softened and I directed his attention towards the representative of the slave master. "This man," I said, "gave you life. Owing to his actions and the fate of your African ancestors, you have this life. Without him, you would not be Caribbean; neither would you have the Dutch and English languages as your own. You owe your life to him." My client stood and moved directly in front of the slave master, tears rolling down his face, and serenely bowed before him. A moment later, when I brought in a representative for his Dutch father, my client's sobs become more intense. His chest heaved and he simply flung his arms around his father's representative saying between his sobs, "Daddy I've missed you." What my client realised was that not only had he rejected his Dutch ancestors who had been responsible for such suffering, but he had also denied his own father in the process, preferring instead to align himself with the victims of slavery.

When we look at such historical events that have touched our ancestors so deeply, it behoves us to realise that such events have created us as we are. Perhaps our mother is from a colony and our father belongs to the land that colonised, perhaps our father is German, and our mother is Jewish, or perhaps our mother is Irish-American and our father's ancestors were Cree, Sioux or Apache. Whichever way we look at it, fate—a force much greater than ourselves—brought our parents together. We often say that every cloud has a silver lining; however, when it comes to the dark clouds of the fate of ancestors, the silver lining is the life we are now leading. If you are a Jewish-American, your life as an American simply would not be if it had not been for the fate of the Pogroms or the Holocaust. If you are an Irish-American, your life may simply not be, were it not for the Irish potato famine. And if you are English, your life, your language and your culture would not be if it weren't for the invasions of the Romans, Saxons and Normans. When we resist the unchangeable fact of where our ancestors are from and what happened to them, we invariably resist our own life. Take a moment to imagine one of your distant ancestors, perhaps one who suffered a difficult fate. Ask yourself this question: Would the Soul of this ancestor want you to deny your own life out of loyalty to him? Or would he want to see you flourish in honour of all your ancestors?

On a more direct and personal level, there are other fates that many of us resist. For example, we resist the fate that our mother died when we were fourteen, we resist the fate that our younger brother was handicapped, we resist the fate our father re-married after our mother's death, or we resist the fate that we are gay or lesbian, or that we are too tall, too thin, or that our hair is red, too curly or just not like our sister's hair. Family Constellation work can take us to a deeply spiritual experience when we bow in submission to our fate, in totality. In essence, in that bodily movement we are living the prayer 'Thy will be done'. Whenever I have observed such a deep, inner movement, the room has been filled with an audible silence; it is truly the presence of Grace.

CHAPTER FOUR

THE CONSTELLATIONS

The following pages contain examples of constellations. With the inclusion of these varied examples, I hope to demonstrate not only the broad scope of Family Constellation work, but also illustrate that none of us are islands immune to the influence of our family groups. I hope to inspire you to broaden your search for solutions to challenges that may beset you—be they physical, mental, emotional or within relationships.

Each of these examples is based on real clients I have worked with, however, names and other details have been changed in order to protect their privacy. The constellation dialogue has been greatly shortened and reduced to its fundamental healing components for the sake of this book, but each gives a snapshot of both the issue and the resolution. What needs to be made clear is that Family Constellation work is neither role-play nor psychodrama, although on the surface it may appear to be so.

A family constellation is set up when members of a group are asked to represent members of a family and are placed intuitively in a standing pattern on the workshop floor. The representatives have little to no information about the individuals they represent, and it is their interaction and presence in the Knowing Field that allows them to take on the feelings of those whom they represent. For representatives, this can become a very intense experience, emotionally as well as physically, as they manifest symptoms as part of the family story.

Prior to a constellation, in order to avoid influencing representatives with too much family story, the bare minimum of information is given during the set-up process. Over the years I have often set up constellations incognito in order to see the results, and have been astounded at the accuracy of the story as it unfolded. However, as reliable as family constellations are in terms of revealing the true story of a family and the events that took place, I strongly discourage that they be used as absolute proof or as an evidence gathering exercise. For example, as an energy, sexual abuse can become evident within a constellation, and can lead to all sorts of conclusions being drawn and false accusations made. However, on many occasions, I have found that although the constellation may appear to indicate that sexual abuse has taken place in the present family of the client, it is often revealed that the energy dynamic is present because it may have happened a generation or two earlier and a residual remains which still has an impact on the family today. I am very cautious about blindly accepting stories of sexual abuse from clients who have gained the memories of such abuse through hypnosis and other forms of regression. When we enter altered states of consciousness, it is very easy for us to read the Knowing Field of the family. In such altered states we can read and feel the energy of sexual abuse, and then our conscious logical mind creates a story and 'memory' that logically fits with the energy experienced.

The question I am most often asked is whether those who are represented but not present in the workshop gain some benefit from this work. The evidence seems to suggest that in many cases they are beneficially influenced in some way. However, at other times, it would seem that the only benefit is for the client who has worked directly with the system.

During Michael's constellation, much work was done to alleviate entanglements in his father's family, which in turn had an influence on Michael himself. When Michael returned home, his father called him and said, "I don't know what happened today, I was out doing some gardening and all of a sudden it felt as if a load had been lifted off my shoulders. I feel great, there must have been some kind of miracle."

I advise each of my clients not to share their constellation stories with their family, but simply enjoy the benefits of the work.

Suzanne had not spoken to her sister for two years after a family argument. Immediately after her family constellation we had a tea break. She walked over to me after some minutes into the break saying excitedly, "You won't believe it, but my sister left voicemail on my cell, and she wants to talk!"

Additionally, there have been occasions when individuals, on hearing about the power of this work, have attended a Family Constellation workshop in order to change another person, either a spouse or a parent. All change starts with us, and when this work is approached with the sole purpose of influencing change in another who is not pursuing this line of healing work, it lacks both respect and integrity and I refuse to work with such clients. However, more often than not, after speaking with them for a couple of minutes, their attitude and approach will change. What is interesting, if not amusing, is that I have often seen women who have dragged their husband along to a workshop, telling me in advance that he has many 'issues', and when it comes to their constellation, it is indeed the wife who has greater resistance and difficulty with the process, as she has a strong need to be right.

Whatever your reason for wanting to enter into Family Constellation work, it can provide you with a snapshot of truth that is undeniable, allowing you to make inner changes in an instant. I encourage you to read the following pages slowly, allowing each of the processes to be absorbed on a deeper level than if you simply skim the pages. Many people report that simply by reading about family constellations or witnessing someone else's process, an inner process towards change starts.

At the end of this book, there is an exercise in which you can put together your own family map that will help you to identify possible areas of healing.

I don't belong

Arnold was a young man in his late twenties who was attracted to Family Constellation work, as he had been struggling with a sense of not belonging and with other destructive patterns.

Payne to Arnold: What would you like to work with?

Arnold: I've been struggling all of my life with a feeling of not belonging. I have few friends and even when I am with friends, I feel as if I am in a bubble, separate from them, locked up in my own little world. Dating and relationships have never been successful as I convince myself ahead of time that they wouldn't want me anyway.

Payne to Arnold: That's quite difficult. Is there anything else?

Arnold: The only thing I seem to excel at is my career. I'm a workaholic and drive myself to perfection all the time. I'm never happy with my performance although my pay raises seem to reflect that my bosses are. I'm so hard on myself.

Payne to Arnold: Did anything in particular happen in your family?

Arnold: No. I've been in therapy before… everything was normal. I have a good relationship with my mum and dad and with my younger sister. It's just this feeling of not belonging. I even feel awkward being here today, I feel that I'm the only one who doesn't belong to this group.

Payne to Arnold: Did anyone die in the family?

Arnold: No, nothing. No one died. Not in my immediate family or in my parent's families.

Payne to Arnold: Were either of your parents previously married, engaged or otherwise in a serious relationship?

Arnold: Only my mother, she was married briefly, then divorced her first husband and married my father.

Payne to Arnold: Well, let's see what is going on. Please choose representatives for yourself, your mother, your father and your sister. We'll also include a representative for your mother's first husband.

Figure 1

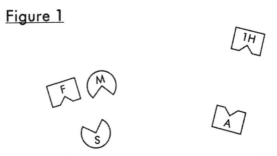

F: Father   M: Mother   S: Sister   A: Arnold   1H: First husband

Payne to Arnold: If we look at this picture, we have the family over to the left, made up of your mother, father and sister, and you have placed both yourself and your mother's first husband far away. Neither of you seem to belong.

Payne to Mother: What's happening here?

Mother: I'm very aware of my son over there, he seems so far away and I can also feel heaviness behind me. Something to do with my first husband, I think.

Payne to Father: So how are things with you?

Father: I'm disturbed that I can't see my son properly; I would rather have him next to me. I'm also aware of the first husband and I'm not comfortable with it.

Payne to Sister: And how are you?

Sister: Agitated. Nervous. There is something missing here. I'm a little irritated too. There's something I can't quite put my finger on, but I can feel it strongly.

Payne to Arnold's Representative: How are you doing over here?

Arnold's Representative: I feel very sad and lonely. In a bubble of sorts, just like Arnold said. I want to go to sleep.

Payne to Arnold: Have you ever been suicidal?

Arnold: Not seriously, I've never planned it or anything, but I often think about death and suicide.

Payne to First Husband: So how are things with you?

First Husband: I can't look up. I feel very heavy.

Payne to Arnold: Something happened in this first marriage. It would appear that someone died. See, he's staring at the ground as if looking into a grave. What happened?

Arnold: My father once told me that my mother had a stillborn baby with her first husband. I've never asked my mother about it. I didn't think it was important and she doesn't like talking about her first marriage.

Payne to Arnold: Was it a boy or a girl?

Arnold: A boy I think. He lived for a few hours only.

Payne to Arnold: Then we must include your older brother.

Payne rearranges the constellation in order to include Arnold's elder brother who died just after birth.

Figure 2

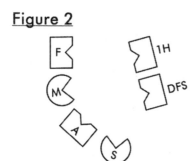

F: Father   M: Mother   A: Arnold   S: Sister   1H: First husband
DFS: Deceased first son

Payne to Father: How is it for you when you see them together like that?

Father: I can't look; I want nothing to do with this. I feel protective of my wife.

Payne to Mother: And how is it for you now that your firstborn son is here with your first husband?

Mother: I can't bear to look at them. It's too painful. I'd rather look at my husband.

Payne to Arnold's Representative: How is it for you?

Arnold's Representative: I feel transfixed by my dead brother. I feel that I know him, almost like a twin.

Payne to Sister: And how are you?

Sister: I feel relieved! But I'm even angrier than before. I'm furious. Maybe at my mother, I don't know, but I'm furious.

Arnold interjects: That sounds just like my sister. She's always angry at my parents, arguing about everything.

Payne to Arnold: Your brother has been forgotten and the constellation shows clearly that you are identified with him. This is the source of your feelings of not belonging, living in a bubble as you put it. Let's see what we can do.

Payne to Mother: Please look directly at your first husband and firstborn son.

Mother: It's overwhelming. I'm not sure that I can.

Payne takes a representative for her mother, Arnold's maternal grandmother, and places her behind her daughter for support.

Figure 3

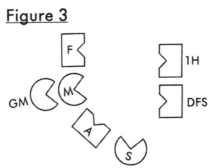

GM: Maternal grandmother   F: Father   M: Mother   S: Sister
A: Arnold   1H: First husband   DFS: Deceased first son

Payne to Mother: How is that now?

Mother: It's easier to face now (begins to sob). It's so sad.

Payne to Mother: Go over and embrace them both.

Mother: I'm not sure that I can. I don't want to leave my husband's side.

Payne to Mother: Well, let's try it anyway.

Mother's representative moves across the floor and embraces her first husband and firstborn son.

Payne to Father: How is that when you see your wife over there?

Father: Difficult. It's sad, and I'm sad for her.

Payne to Mother: Look at your firstborn son and say to him, "I take you as my son and give you a place in my heart."

Mother: I take you as my son and give you a place in my heart.

Payne to Firstborn Son: How does that feel to hear your mother say that?

Firstborn Son: I feel that I finally belong. It feels good to be acknowledged.

Payne to Mother: Now look at your first husband and say, "It's a great pity that things went the way that they did between us, for I loved you. This was a difficult fate for both of us."

Mother to First Husband: It's a great pity that things went the way that they did between us, for I loved you. This was a difficult fate for both of us.

Mother and first husband spontaneously embrace and mourn together.

Payne to Mother: Now stand between your first husband and firstborn son and say to your other son and daughter, "This is your brother, the firstborn, he has his place."

Mother: This is your brother, the firstborn. He has his place.

Payne to the other Children: How does that feel?

Arnold's Representative: It feels good. I miss him.

Sister: My anger has completely gone now, but I feel sad.

Payne to Children: Come and meet your brother.

The representatives for Arnold and his sister cross the floor and embrace their brother for the first time.

Firstborn Son: This feels wonderful. I have a family.

Payne to Arnold's Representative and Sister: Say to your brother, "It's a great pity that you couldn't stay, because we've missed you. We take you as our eldest brother."

Payne rearranges the constellation to reflect the resolved family structure and replaces Arnold's Representative with the client Arnold.

Figure 4

1H: First husband   F: Father   M: Mother
FB: Deceased firstborn   A: Arnold   S: Sister

Payne to Arnold: How does that feel now?

Arnold: It's the first time in my life that I feel that I belong. May I go over and hug my brother?

Payne to Arnold: Not only may you do that, it's encouraged.

Arnold embraces his brother and the two men are very moved.

Payne to Arnold: Say to your brother, "Dear Brother, although you did not live, I shall live my life fully in honour of you. Wait patiently for me, for one day we shall be together when it is my proper time."

Arnold: Dear Brother, although you did not live, I shall live my life fully in honour of you. Wait patiently for me, for one day we shall be together when it is my proper time.

Payne to Arnold: Now say, "Smile upon me kindly and bless all that I have."

Arnold: Smile upon me kindly and bless all that I have.

Payne to Arnold: How does that feel?

Arnold: It's a relief, so much pressure off my shoulders.

Payne to Firstborn Son: And for you?

Firstborn Son: (smiling broadly) It's a relief for me too. I'm happy for him.

Constellation concludes.

Payne to Arnold: Do you understand your drive to be perfect now?

Arnold: Not quite.

Payne: You've been trying to live your brother's life as well, trying to be two sons, twice as perfect and twice as lonely. Take the final picture into your Soul and think fondly of your brother, respecting his fate.

Arnold: That strikes a chord. It explains my obsession and drive. Thank you.

Conclusion

The most difficult and challenging event for any couple to face is the loss of a child, especially if it is a firstborn infant. When a heterosexual couple falls in love and has a view towards marriage, children often symbolise the consummation of that love. It is part of their dream of family and parenthood, the continuation of themselves and their love through their children. When a child is lost in this way, that dream is shattered and the marriage more often than not breaks down along with it. Additionally, the pain of losing an infant is such a deep one, that parents cannot look at their child or accept the fate of the child, even their own fate as parents. In this way, stillborn children and infants who have died become excluded. This exclusion leads to representation by another within the family system, in order to once again bring balance. In Arnold's case, he was identified with his elder brother, not only taking on the feelings associated with being cast out or forgotten, but also trying to lead his brother's life by being 'doubly perfect'. This is a great burden. What we have observed through family constellations is that hierarchy is important to the flow and Orders of Love. Arnold saw himself as the firstborn in the family, when in fact his brother belonged to the system as the firstborn, although of a different father. Seeing himself as the firstborn, when indeed he is the second, would give him the feeling of 'not fitting in' or 'not having a place in the world'. I would like to mention here that although Arnold's brother was in fact his half-brother, I discourage the terms 'half-brother' and 'half-sister' as they appear to diminish the sense of belongingness and importance of siblings.

Having worked in the Caribbean, the U.S., and Africa, it is interesting to note that in Afro-Caribbean, Afro-American and some African cultures, many people only consider another as their brother or sister if they are born to the same mother, whilst not acknowledging other children born to the same father. Through Family Constellations, I have observed that when all of the children of both mother and father are included, each child ultimately feels strengthened by this. This is the legacy of African slavery and apartheid, where men and women were forcibly kept apart, not allowed to form established family units. This led to casual encounters or relationships that were separated by force of law, which led to mothers giving birth to several children, each or most from different fathers. When boys in particular are separated from their father, they have no sense of support and do not feel that they fully belong to the world of men. This in turn leads to the pattern of single mother families and men who have children with several partners repeating for many generations. Many Caucasian Americans, Caribbeans and South Africans are very critical of this aspect of African-origin culture without understanding the impact of the actions their own ancestors have had upon many African peoples. While some point out that this phenomenon is relatively new, my observation of families of African descent has shown me that the church and religion have stood in place for the missing fathers of the past, the Holy Father and Jesus, both paternal symbols, taking their place. With the gradual evaporation of the importance of religion, the church no longer represents the missing father, so the pattern now re-emerges with force. We have also observed that systemic problems can, and very often do, skip several generations.

Caroline

Caroline entered family constellation work feeling that she was in deep emotional crisis. Her marriage was breaking down and her lifelong feeling of not belonging had risen to the surface in a way that was controlling her life. Caroline revealed that prior to her own birth, her parents had another daughter who died of illness just months before Caroline was born. Her sister was just under two when she died, and had also been called Caroline. Being named after her dead, firstborn sister was a great burden for Caroline; she constantly felt that she had no right to be herself, but had to fill her sister's shoes and live up to that role. Similarly, I have worked with cases where a child has been named after either the mother's or the father's first love who may have died tragically, or after some other family member who had an untimely or tragic death. Even though these children may not be aware consciously that they have been named after a missing person, they still feel it and it becomes a heavy burden for them. When we name children after those who are missing from the family system, we are in effect asking these children to replace them. This does not allow them to feel their own place in the world, making it difficult for them to get in contact with who they truly are.

When there is a family tradition of naming children after grandparents, problems only arise if the grandparent in question died at a young age. For example, if your mother died when you were a child, it is not prudent to name your own daughter after her, for it can lead to systemic entanglement where the relationship between mother and daughter is not clearly defined.

What's in a name?

I was once asked to set up a constellation as a proxy for a young man who was sitting in jail awaiting trial on drug charges. The representative for this young man reported that he had strong feelings of not belonging and of being worthless. When his parents divorced, his mother moved to a new country taking my client and his brother with her. They had no further contact with their father. The mother, out of not wanting to have anything to do with her former husband—the father of the boys—changed not only their surname, *but also their first names*, for the father had named the boys at birth. In effect, the mother's message was 'any part of your father is not good'. The boys felt this deeply and deemed themselves to be not good enough. This is a tragic story of how some children are held hostage by their parents' resentment towards one another.

Gail

Gail was frustrated with her life as she had been in a pattern of changing jobs frequently and ending relationships, always feeling that it wasn't her place, or that she didn't belong. On investigating her family, it transpired that her mother's first pregnancy was miscarried. The constellation revealed that this had a deep impact on her parents and that the family never felt complete. In the constellation, we placed a representative for the miscarried child in the position of firstborn child. Gail felt relieved and felt her place in the family. She was no longer the firstborn, but the second child, which brought balance and harmony.

Having given the example above, it is not to say that all miscarriages are significant, but in my observation, all miscarriages *can* be significant, irrespective of when they happened and the order in which they fall. However, constellation work seems to suggest that the likelihood of impact on the family system is increased manyfold if that miscarriage is the first pregnancy of a relationship. Like any firstborn, this pregnancy symbolises the consummation of the couple's love and the beginnings of family.

My children are very distant

Amanda is 48 years old and has two children. She rarely sees her 23-year-old son and has a strained relationship with her 19-year-old daughter who still lives with her.

Payne to Client: Where is their father? You didn't mention him.

Client: We divorced when my son was 10 and my daughter was 6.

Payne to Client: Why did you divorce?

Client: He left me for another woman.

Payne to Client: What happened?

Client: He started having an affair, then he left one day to move in with her.

Payne to Client: So you are still angry with him, that's clear to see. What else happened between you?

Client: Nothing I can think of, we seemed to have a very normal marriage.

Payne to Client: Well, let's see. Choose representatives for your husband, your son, your daughter and yourself.

Figure 1

Payne to Client: The picture is very clear to see. Your son stands with his father, which is natural if you are angry with his father. Children will almost always be loyal to the parent who is least respected. Look at your daughter. She looks as if she is caught in the middle. But let's find out what it really going on shall we?

Payne to Daughter: How are things here?

Daughter: Exactly as I just heard you say. I don't know where I belong, not to my father and not to my mother. I feel stuck in the middle, it feels terrible, and I feel alone.

Payne to Son: And how are things here?

Son: Fine, I like standing next to my father.

Payne to Son: Look at your mother for a moment, how is that?

Son: I don't really want to look at her. I get angry when I do.

Payne to Husband: How are things here?

Husband: Actually OK, I have my son next to me, which is good, but I am concerned for my daughter, I wish she could be closer.

Payne to Amanda: (noticing that her arms are crossed over her chest) How are things here?

Amanda: I'm angry with my husband. I'm not happy with my son over there, and I want my daughter right next to me, she belongs here (pointing to a place on her left).

Payne moves husband next to Amanda and stands the children side-by-side in front of them at a little distance.

Figure 2

F = Father
M = Mother
D = Daughter
S = Son

Payne to Daughter: How is that?

Daughter: Phew, I'm out of the 'hot seat'; it feels good to be next to my brother.

Payne to Son: How is that for you?

Son: It's good to have my sister next to me, but I still want my father next to me.

Payne to Amanda: How is this for you?

Amanda: I don't want to look at him!

Payne to Husband: How is it for you?

Husband: It's OK, I can look at her, but I don't have any particular feeling.

Payne to Amanda: Look at your husband and say, "It's a great pity that things went the way that they did, because I loved you very much."

Amanda: I can't say that, I'm still too angry.

Payne to Amanda: Let's just try. Just say the words and see what happens.

Amanda to Husband: It's a great pity that things went the way that they did… (Amanda sobs)… because I loved you very much."

Payne to Client: How is this for you when you hear your representative say these words?

Client: It's true, I loved that man deeply, and I still do.

Payne to Client: Let's see if we can find a way so that your children don't have to pay the price for your pain and anger. Shall we?

Payne replaces Amanda's representative with the Amanda the client.

Payne to Client: Say to your husband, "It's a great pity that things went the way that they did, because I loved you very much."

Client: It's a great pity that things went the way that they did, because I loved you very much.

Payne to Client: Now say to him, "I take all that was good between us and give it a special place in my heart."

Client: I take all that was good between us and give it a special place in my heart.

The representative for Amanda's husband smiles and spontaneously places an arm around Amanda's shoulder. They look like a couple now.

Payne to Son: How is this for you?

Son: It's good to see them together, the tension has gone.

Payne to Daughter: How is this for you when you see them together like that, as parents?

Daughter: It's much better, but I'm still a little unsettled.

Payne to Mother: Say this to your daughter, "I honour the part of your father that I see alive in you, and it's good to see."

Mother to Daughter: I honour the part of your father that I see alive in you, and it's good to see.

Payne to Daughter: How is that now?

Daughter: That's a relief, I needed to hear that (sobbing), I love my father very much, and my mother, it was so difficult to love him, I felt trapped.

Payne to Son: How is that for you?

Son: That was good to hear, I needed to hear it, too.

Mother spontaneously says to Son: I honour the part of your father that I see alive in you, and it's good to see.

Payne to Son: And now?

Son: Now I can trust my mother, everything is OK, and I want to be close to both of them.

Payne to both Parents: Say to your children, "Whatever happened between us, leave it with us. It has nothing to do with you, and together we are still the parents."

Parents to Children: Whatever happened between us, leave it with us. It has nothing to do with you, and together we are still the parents.

Payne to Client: How does that feel now?

Client: My heart is still sore, but it feels much better. It's true, my son was becoming more and more like his father, and I shunned him in a way.

Payne to Client: Finally, one more thing to say to your husband, "Thank you for the gift of our children, I honour the part of you I see alive in them."

Client to Husband: Thank you for the gift of our children, I honour the part of you I see alive in them.

Husband spontaneously to Client: Thank you for the gift of our children, I honour the part of you I see alive in them.

Payne to Client: Let me give you some homework to do, Amanda. Go home and think of all the positive qualities that your ex-husband has, the ones that made you fall in love with him and helped you to continue loving him for all of these years. The next time you see your son and you notice that he displays the same or similar qualities say to him something like this, "You know, your father is like that too, and it's good to see." It is important to name the positive quality, don't overdo it, just gracefully bring it into the conversation.

Exercise for Divorced and Separated Parents

Write up a list of the all the positive qualities of your former partner that contributed to you falling in love with them. Take a moment to remember those special qualities.

Now write up a list for all of the positive qualities that you see in your children.

Once you have your two lists, mark the positive qualities and characteristics that are common to both lists. In doing this, you will see more clearly the special gift that your former partner has given you with these children. If you have been holding feelings of resentment, bitterness and anger, or have been involved with disputes with your former partner, the chances are that your children will feel shamed in some way. Memorise these lists and the next opportunity you have, gently praise your child for one of these qualities, and you will be on your way to undoing the shame. Be subtle and discreet, making your comment a part of general conversation. This way the child will receive the message more fully. Children need to know that they were born out of love. Additionally, when you are hostile to a former partner, children experience that either as hostility towards them, or as disapproval. At all costs we should avoid children paying the price for our own unresolved issues with former partners.

Conclusion

The issue that Amanda brought to the constellation work is one that is very often seen in the case of divorced or separated couples who have children. Children will almost always be loyal to the parent who is least respected. What we have learned from such constellations is that irrespective of the father's (or mother's) infidelity, it has nothing to do with the children; it is a private matter between the parents. However, we often see that the party who feels most wounded, will demand loyalty from the children and expect them to take sides. This invariably backfires and the children will either feel torn, or their loyalty will go to the other party, the one who is least respected. At times, we do see that the influence of the wounded party can be so strong that children, no matter their age, feel they don't have permission to love the other parent.

Justin

Justin was 36 years old and his fiancée had just left him. His parents divorced when he was 10 years old. He explained that his father was a womaniser and drank fairly heavily, although there had not been any violence in the family. When he set up his constellation, he placed himself directly next to his mother. It became very clear that he had no permission to love his father and that he had taken his father's place within the family. When we looked at the influence of this set-up on his relationships with women, it was clear that he was not truly free to marry, as he already had a wife in the form of his mother. In such instances, I refer to this scenario as 'emotional incest'. Justin had taken his father's place and he had become the primary emotional relationship for his mother, making it difficult for him to break free. This also happens between father and daughter, but more often if the mother has died, rather than as a result of divorce. However, this kind of father/daughter relationship can also exist when a marriage remains intact, owing to the mother's attention being drawn elsewhere.

Within constellation work, we often work beyond the scope of the problem that has been presented. For example, with Justin, we set up constellations that involved his mother's family of origin in order to disentangle Justin from his mother's own systemic entanglements. This in turn allowed Justin to be free.

Every time I create something good in my life, it simply falls apart

David was a man in his mid-forties. His motivation for attending the workshop was that he felt his life had been cursed in some way. His life had been a pattern of great successes followed by bankruptcies, failed marriages, bad health and bouts of depression.

Payne to David, the Client: Why do you feel that your life has been cursed in some way?

Client: Everything I touch seems to go sour. I've been a millionaire twice, and on both occasions I found myself bankrupt almost overnight. If I buy a new car, it ends up getting recalled by the manufacturer; if I buy a new home, there's a flood, burglaries, you name it, it all goes horribly wrong.

Payne to Client: All these things have happened just once, or have they been happening for a long time?

Client: For as long as I remember. Even relationships are a disaster. My first girlfriend left me for my best friend, my first wife simply disappeared one day—no explanation, another woman stole money from me, and employees also steal money from me. I've had corrupt accountants and lawyers who take money from me. I'm losing faith in life and in people. Sometimes I just feel like dying.

Payne to Client: I often see this kind of life pattern when an individual feels loyal to someone within the family system who has either died young or has suffered a great injustice. Is there anything like this in your family?

Client: Not as far as I know.

Payne to Client: Tell me about your family.

David explained that he came from a fairly wealthy, southern family from Georgia in the USA. He stated his parents, especially his father, were very conservative. During our initial interview, it was revealed that this pattern of sudden failure was also a common theme with other family members. He named an uncle, a couple of cousins and his older sister who had also struggled through life despite the fact that they came from a wealthy home and had a good university education.

Payne to Client: Well let's just see where it comes from, then we can investigate further, shall we?

Payne instructs David to select a representative for his father and mother and place them standing side-by-side on the workshop floor.

Payne to Father: How are things here?

Father: I feel aggressive.

Payne to Father: Yes, I see that your fists are clenched.

Payne to Mother: How are things here?

Mother: (shrugs her shoulders) OK I guess, nothing much. A little curious about my husband, but nothing much.

Payne to Client: So tell me more about your father's family.

Client: I've told you everything I know. I don't know of any early deaths, injustice, or tragedies. I really don't know anything.

Payne to Client: Well let's test this and see what happens.

Payne selects representatives for David's grandfather and great-grandfather and places them in a row directly behind the father.

Figure 1

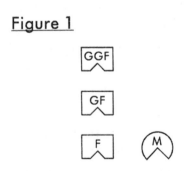

F: Father   GF: Grandfather   GGF: Great Grandfather
M: Mother

Payne to Grandfather: How are things here?

Grandfather: My hands are also clenched into a fist. I'm happy to see my son in front of me, but I also feel aggressive.

Payne to Great-Grandfather: How are things here with you?

Great-Grandfather: I feel very aggressive, plus there's something terrible behind me. I feel a mixture of aggression, violence and fear.

Payne chooses a representative for the great-great-grandfather and places him behind the great-grandfather.

Payne to Great-Grandfather: How is this now, with your father behind you?

Great-Grandfather: It's worse, I'm more afraid, but at the same time feel more violent. It's terrible having him here.

Payne to all the other representatives: Did it get better or worse when great-great-grandfather came in?

Grandfather: Much worse, it's not aggression any longer, it's violence.

Father: I feel like running, I'm afraid.

Mother: I can hardly breathe; it's terrible since he came in. I was fairly disinterested, but I'm totally involved now that he is here.

Payne to Client: Does any of this make sense to you?

Client: In a way, they were all so strict. The violence is puzzling to me though.

Payne to Client: Tell me about great-great-grandfather, what do you know?

Client: Oh, quite a bit. He owned a lot of land, he was a plantation owner, and so was my great-grandfather. The land was lost after my great-grandmother committed suicide and my great-grandfather lost most of his money and land to gambling debts and alcoholism.

Payne to Client: So, your family owned plantations? Did they own slaves?

Client: Yes, they owned many slaves.

Payne instructs David to select representatives for his great-grandmother who committed suicide, a representative for himself and one or more representatives for African slaves according to his feelings. He was also instructed to rearrange the constellation according to his own feelings, if need be.

Figure 2

GGGF: Great Greatgrandfather GGF: Great Grandfather
GGM: Great Grandmother S1: Slave S2: Slave D: David

Note that David is standing right next to the representatives for the slaves and that both his great-grandfather and great-great-grandfather are facing the opposite way. Great-grandmother is looking directly at the slaves. His mother has been moved to a position just on the periphery of the constellation, also looking away. David's father is looking at his wife, as if following her.

Payne to David's Representative: How does it feel here?

David's Representative: Terrible. I feel nauseous and full of shame and guilt.

Payne to Client: Does that make sense to you?

Client: Yes, I know these feelings very well. I've felt guilty all of my life.

Payne to Client: Well, let's work a little further and see what we can do. It seems as if you are carrying your family guilt. This story may explain your great-grandmother's suicide. Strange that you didn't mention it in the initial interview.

Client: I didn't think it was important, it seems so far away.

Payne to Client: When we look at this picture, it seems very close to you.

Client: Yes, I feel all sorts of things going on inside of me now.

Payne to Mother: What's going on here?

Mother: This has got nothing to do with me, I'd rather look out here (she points to the far side of the room).

Payne to Father: How are things here?

Father: I want to be with my wife. I really don't want to look at this. It's easier to be with her.

Payne to Great-Grandmother: How are things with you?

Great-Grandmother: I'm confused. I feel very sick, like vomiting. I don't belong to this family; I want to be with them (she points to the slaves).

Payne turns the representatives for great-grandfather and great-great-grandfather around so that they can see the slaves and David's representative next to them. He also turns the mother and father around so that they can face the picture.

Figure 3

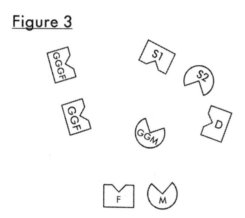

GGGF: Great Greatgrandfather GGF: Great Grandfather
GGM: Great Grandmother S1: Slave S2: Slave D: David
F: Father M: Mother

Payne to Great-Great-Grandfather: How are things here when we turn you around?
Great-Great Grandfather: OK I guess.
Payne to Great-Great-Grandfather: Look directly at your slaves.
Great-Great-Grandfather: I don't want to.
Payne to Great-Great-Grandfather: You may not want to, but I'm asking you to.
Payne to Great-Grandfather: Please join your father and look directly at the slaves.
Great-Grandfather: I really don't want to. And I won't do it just because you are telling me to.
Payne to Great-Grandfather: OK, then look at your father as he looks at the slaves.

The constellation is left in silence for several minutes, simply waiting for a movement of the Soul to transpire. After several minutes, great-great-grandfather falls to his knees in front of the slaves and exclaims, "What have I done?" Great-grandfather joins his father and sobs heavily.

Payne to Great-Grandmother: How are things with you now?

Great-Grandmother: Very, very sad, but my sick feeling has gone. I feel relieved.

Payne to David's Representative: How do you feel now?

David's Representative: I feel an overwhelming sense of sadness, it's almost too much to bear.

Payne to Mother and Father: And how are things for you now?

Father: Very sad.

Mother: Very sad, and concerned for my son.

Payne to the Slaves: How are you doing?

Female Slave: I felt terrible in the beginning, but now I also feel sad, for them and for us. Strangely, I feel warm towards these people. I'm glad it's over.

Male Slave: I was angry, aggressive and deeply grieved in the beginning, now I feel at peace (he looks at the great-great-grandfather). I want to help this man up to his feet.

Payne to Great-Great-Grandfather: Look at your great-great-grandson and say to him, "This guilt is mine, all of it. I alone carry the consequences. Leave it with me."

Great-Great-Grandfather: This guilt is mine, all of it. I alone carry the consequences. Leave it with me.

David's Representative: It's a relief.

Payne takes out David's representative and replaces him with the client David.

Payne to Client: Say to your Great-Great-Grandfather, "I respectfully leave it with you" and bow your head as you do so.

Client: I respectfully leave it with you.

Payne to Client: How does that feel?

Client: Like the guilt I've felt all of these years is being washed away.

Payne to Client: Now look directly at the slaves.

Client: (sobbing) It all makes sense now. When I was rich, I often gave a lot of money to charities, especially to an African-American College fund. May I embrace them?

Payne to Client: Yes, you may, and say to the slaves, "Yours was a difficult fate, I shall now live my life fully in honour of you. I give you a place in my heart."

Client: Yours was a difficult fate, I shall now live my life fully in honour of you. I give you a place in my heart.

It is interesting to note here, that as David said "I shall now live my life fully in honour of you" the representatives for the slaves gave a sigh of relief and smiled at him. Their Souls were now at peace.

Conclusion

Whenever I see a constellation like this, I am reminded of the Bible saying, 'The sins of the father will be visited upon the son'. It is not that some external source is punishing future generations, but that such heavy burdens of guilt associated with injustice and ill-gotten gain are carried by the entire family Soul and passed down from one generation to the next. However, it is important to say that this happens when the perpetrators do not accept responsibility for their acts. As the Soul seeks to include all that is excluded, even guilt, as balance is sought, it will simply be carried by another member of the family.

As in David's story, a family's success followed by great loss, various individuals who could not make a success of their lives, gambling debts, alcoholism, even suicides, are fairly typical results of similar historical events. Such patterns can be found anywhere colonisation, forced labour, slavery and ill treatment of native peoples have taken place. I've seen these patterns emerging in the southern states of the USA, in South Africa, among some Australians, Dutch Indonesians, Caribbeans, and British and French Colonialist families.

Conversely, I've worked with a number of individuals who have the same pattern of self-sabotage, but in their case, they are the descendants of those who have suffered. For example, people of Native American, Jewish and African-American ancestry, as well as Coloured South Africans and other people of mixed race sometimes develop this pattern of not living life fully, out of loyalty to those who have suffered greatly. Their inner feeling is that they have no right to live fulfilled lives as those who gave them life have suffered so much. Such loyalties are at times difficult bonds to break. However, what constellation work has shown over and over, is that the dead feel relieved and happy when the bond of guilt has been broken; then they are free to fulfill their natural role of being a source of strength, rather than of weakness.

Constellations such as David's are truly trans-generational in nature, which in itself can pose problems to individuals with similar issues in their lives when entering therapy. When a therapist is engaged to assist with issues of self-sabotage, most work deals directly with childhood experiences and issues within the family. Although some good can come out of this work, unless a therapist understands the nature of family systems and trans-generational transference, a client may spend much time and money in therapy and never uncover the root cause of the problem. It is worth noting here that when David was asked directly if there were any cases of injustice or tragic deaths in his family, he failed to mention the history of slavery in his family or his great-grandmother's suicide. Many clients have what I call 'spontaneous memory'. I can ask them very specific questions about very specific events and people when preparing to work with them and they give me little or no information. However, once the Knowing Field is activated through setting up a constellation, suddenly they remember vital details that evaded them earlier. It has happened on numerous occasions that I've asked someone, "Have there been any tragic deaths in the family?" and the answer comes back, "No." Then, just a few minutes into a constellation I ask, "Your mother seems very sad, what happened here?" and the client replies, "She had a stillborn baby two years before I was born." What this reveals is not human failings in terms of our ability to remember, but rather how family groups choose, consciously or otherwise, to forget tragedy and death.

George

George was interested in Family Constellation work. He was initially attracted to the work as he was investigating a number of alternative avenues for dealing with his many health issues, HIV being one of them. George had attended workshops about six or seven times, had read some books on the topic and had enthusiastically asked me lots of questions about family systems. On his seventh or eighth visit, I stopped mid-constellation and asked him, "There seems to be someone missing?". George replied, "Oh yes, my father was married before and he has a daughter, my older sister." Despite seeing dozens of family systems being set up and participating as representative on numerous occasions, George failed to mention that he even had a sister or that his father had been married prior to marrying his mother. However, it is also important to mention here that when George's elder sister was brought into his constellation, there was stubborn refusal on the part of George to accept her as the 'first' and himself as the 'second', which in turn highlighted other issues. What this example illustrates is that all of us, at one time or another are guilty of making others 'less than' and excluding them from the family system, whether deliberately or on a subtler, sub-conscious level.

Whenever anyone or anything is excluded, we see consequences within the family system. Family secrets especially can have a deep residual impact on an entire family system for several generations. The nature of the Soul is to be equal to and inclusive of all things. This applies to both the individual Soul and the Soul of a family, which is the collective conscience, and consciousness, of a biological family group spanning many generations.

Allen

Beverley, a Jewish woman in her late thirties came to me for assistance. She described her 14-year-old son as being 'totally out of control'. She was very inquisitive about new ways of thinking and had been told that Allen was an 'Indigo Child', meaning that he was a highly-evolved, sensitive Soul who found this world difficult to deal with. My experience tells me that highly-evolved Souls don't generally behave in such ways and that I'd rather find the answer within the family than look at celestial meanings behind a child's behaviour.

I learnt that most of Beverley's husband's family had died in the Holocaust and her family had lost some relatives as well. They kept a largely kosher household, and out of loyalty to their parents and grandparents, did not buy or use any German products. In setting up constellations, neither parent—especially Allen's father—could even look at representatives for the Germans, exclaiming, "They are not human." Allen's representative, on the other hand, stood right next to the representative for a camp commandant. In order to solve this problem, I brought in representatives for the camp commandant's wife and children and had Beverley and a representative for her husband look at them and say, "Like us, you, too, are human." It was only when his parents could give a place in their hearts to the Germans—even the Nazis—could Allen stand next to them.

When we look at examples like this, it is clear that not only will victims—the forgotten and guilty—be represented in the family, but also the perpetrators. Allen's parents totally disowned the Germans and the Nazis, seeing them as less than human, and were unable to have anything German in their home. On a deeper level, Allen was compelled to represent the Nazis in his family through displaying 'out of control' behaviour. This is the nature of the Soul, it seeks to include that which has been excluded and disowned.

I often feel suicidal

Michael is a young, gay man of 26. He explained that for as long as he can remember, he always felt depressed and often had thoughts of suicide. He also explained that he was a frequent user of marijuana as this helped him to 'escape'. He had never been in therapy previously and was motivated to join Family Constellation work through a friend who had attended several workshops.

Payne to Michael, the Client: Did anyone die young in your family?

Client: No one in the immediate family, my mother didn't lose any children or anything. But her mother died when she was eight years old.

Payne to Client: Were there special circumstances surrounding your grandmother's death?

Client: She died of cancer and was ill for more than a year.

Payne to Client: Tell me about your father's side of the family, any early or tragic deaths there?

Client: Not as far as I know, my grandparents are still alive and I visit them regularly.

Payne to Client: Well, let's set it up. Choose representatives for your mother, her mother, your father and yourself.

Figure 1

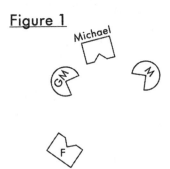

Payne to Client: I see that your representative is standing right next to your grandmother, away from your father and mother. Isn't that a little strange?

Client: Yes, but it felt right at the time I placed them. I don't know why, I just wanted to stand next to my grandmother. I didn't even know her; she died a long time before I was born.

Payne steps into the constellation and starts interviewing the representatives about their feelings.

Payne to Mother: How are things here?

Mother: I can't bear to look at my mother, it's terrible (she sobs).

Payne to Mother: What happens if you look at her directly?

Mother: I want to go to her, but I'm afraid, my body is trembling inside.

Payne to Mother: And when you look at your son next to her?

Mother: (looks surprised by the question) I didn't even notice him there. I didn't realise that I had a son.

Payne to Father: How are things here?

Father: I'm not part of this. My wife can't even see me, and I can't see my son properly. I don't really seem to belong here.

Payne to Michael's Representative: How are things here?

Michael's Representative: Mixed feelings. I feel that I am supposed to stand here next to my grandmother, and I feel very, very sad if I look at her, but I am also worried that I can't really see my father.

Payne asks representative for the grandmother to lie flat on her back on the floor, eyes closed, as if dead. Mother's representative falls to her knees almost immediately and Michael's representative sobs audibly. The father's representative also wipes a tear from his eye.

Payne to Mother: What is happening now?

Mother: It's terrible (wipes away tears), I have a deep longing for her, it's so painful, I want to go to her.

Payne instructs the mother to follow her feelings and honour what her body tells her to do. She slowly moves across and lies next to her mother, as if dead.

Figure 2

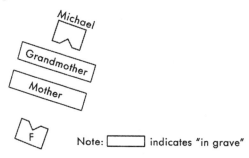

Note: ▭ indicates "in grave"

Payne to Mother: How are things now?

Mother: I am at peace; it's good to be with her.

Payne to Michael: And how are things now for you?

Michael: I want to lie down with them…but now I can see my father. I feel stuck here, I don't know what to do.

Payne moves Michael's Representative to stand next to his father. The father breathes a sigh of relief.

Figure 3

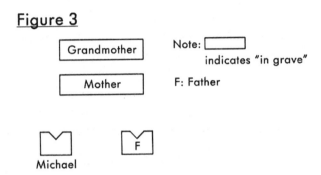

Michael: It feels better, but I'm still drawn to go to them.

Payne turns to client and says, "Hence your draw to marijuana. You are caught between two worlds, neither here, nor there (pointing towards those laying in the graves). The client sobs as he takes in the clear picture. Payne replaces Michael's representative with the client Michael.

Payne to Client: How does it feel here?

Client: He doesn't like me because I am gay.

Payne to Client: From what I can see, he felt isolated; you and your mother were with your dead grandmother and not with him.

Representative nods in agreement and smiles at client.

Payne to Father: Say to your son, "It's much safer next to me. You belong here at my side."

Father: (looking directly into his son's eyes) It's much safer next to me. You belong here at my side.

The two embrace and Michael the client exclaims, "I've missed my father so much" and sobs on his father's shoulder.

Conclusion

Michael's mother could not look at her dead mother. In this way, she excluded her mother through not being able to accept her difficult fate. Additionally, as Michael's mother did not even recognise that she had a son, Michael, in part, felt compelled to stand next to his grandmother so that he could be seen. His mother was very drawn to the world of the dead, and was herself suicidal. In this way, Michael could be seen by his mother if he, too, stood in the world of the dead.

Very often, when a parent dies early, the child who is left behind has a very strong urge to follow. In this instance, it was clear that Michael's mother was suicidal and wanted to follow her mother into the grave. Michael had taken on his mother's feelings and wanted to be with the dead as his mother could not see the living. I suspect that Michael, who is a very effeminate gay man, also represented his grandmother in the family by taking on such feminine characteristics. This is a difficult fate, feeling unseen unless you live the life of one who has died before you.

Michael reports that his marijuana use declined rapidly over a period of two months directly after the constellation and now he rarely uses it. Additionally, he is now building a healthy relationship with his father, one in which his sexuality rarely seems to be an issue any longer.

Not sure if I want to marry or not

Patricia is a young woman in her early thirties. She attended a workshop, as she wanted to get clear about her relationship and her resistance to marrying a man whom, she stated, clearly loved her. During her interview, I asked if she had any previous, serious relationships. She revealed that she had been engaged to a Frenchman but had left him.

Payne instructs Patricia to set up the constellation choosing representatives for herself, her current fiancé, and her former fiancé. She sets up the constellation where her representative is looking directly at both men.

Figure 1

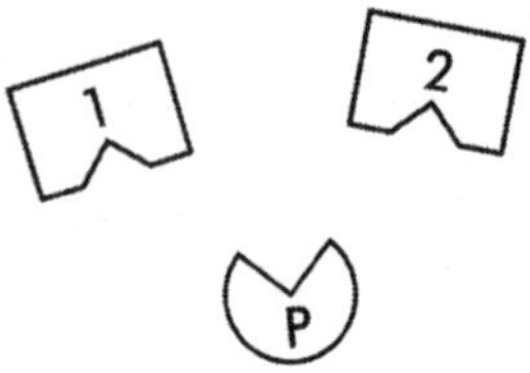

1: Current Fiancé   2: Former Fiancé   3: Patricia

Payne to Patricia's Representative: How are things here?

Patricia's Representative: I can't choose between them.

Payne to Patricia: Look at your former fiancé directly and tell me how you feel.

Patricia: Now that you ask me to look at him directly, I find it difficult. I feel a mixture of sadness and remorse.

Payne turns to Client: What happened here?

Client: I don't know. We were in love, about to get married, and I left. No real reason (she sobs), he was a wonderful man.

Payne to Client: Were there any pregnancies? Did he have a former partner?

Client: No, neither. We were young.

Payne to Patricia: Move closer to him, stand right in front of him and look at him.

Patricia: When I get closer, I feel an urge to leave him. When I stand back, I feel love, remorse and sadness. Up close I feel the need to run.

Payne to Client: Did either your mother or father have a former lover before marrying each other?

Client: Yes, my mother.

Payne: What happened?

Client: My mother left him, although she loved him. She still speaks of him from time to time.

Payne: Anyone else?

Client: My grandmother. She also left her fiancé.

Payne: Do you know why your grandmother did this?

Client: Yes, he was also French, like my fiancé. Her parents were well-to-do from Holland. They didn't allow her to marry him because he was Catholic. My grandmother was raised in a fairly strict Protestant household.

Payne brings in representatives for the mother, grandmother and their respective fiancés.

Figure 2

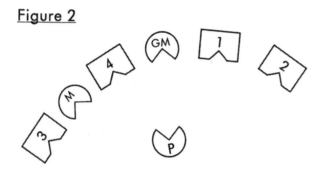

1: Current Fiancé   2: Former Fiancé   3: Mother's Fiancé
4: Grandmother's Fiancé   P: Patricia

The representative for Patricia's grandmother weeps profusely and reports that she is so grief-stricken that she wants to fall to her knees, she can hardly stand.

Payne to Patricia: How is it when you see you grandmother?
Patricia: It's terrible. I have a pain in my chest, my heart hurts, I'm so sad. None of the women in my family marry the men they love.
Payne to Patricia: Turn and look at your former fiancé.
Patricia: (overcome with grief, sobbing) I've never loved anyone like I love this man.
Payne to Patricia: Now look at your mother.
Patricia: It's the same feeling. I feel overwhelmed with sadness for my mother.

Payne brings in representatives for Patricia's grandmother's parents and places them behind her. Also, without naming it, he places a representative for the church next to them. Often in family constellations, in order to avoid unnecessary projection on the part of representatives or simply to test theories, representatives can be brought in without them knowing who they are. The Knowing Field works in exactly the same way with accurate feelings and motivations that naturally come to the surface irrespective of conscious knowledge of who or what they represent.

Figure 3

1: Current Fiancé   2: Former Fiancé   3: Mother's Fiancé
4: Grandmother's Fiancé   GGF: Great Grandfather
GGM: Great Grandmother   ⚰ Church   P: Patricia

Payne asks representative for mother to turn and look at her parents.

Payne to Grandmother: How is it when you look at your parents?

Grandmother: I don't really want to look at them, it's very difficult.

Payne to Great-Grandmother: How is it when your daughter tries to look at you and can't?

Great-Grandmother: I have a mixture of feelings. Stubbornness, guilt and sadness. All the feelings are mixed, none stronger than the other.

Payne to Great-Grandfather: How is it when you look at your daughter?

Great-Grandfather: I don't really want to look at her, I'd rather turn away.

Payne to Great-Grandfather: Say to you daughter, "I did it for the Church."

Great-Grandfather: I did it for the Church.

The grandmother looks visibly angry when she hears her father say this.

Payne to the Church: So how are things here when you see this story?

Church: (shrugs shoulders) I don't belong here, I don't know these people.

Payne asks grandmother to face her granddaughter.

Payne to Grandmother: Say to your granddaughter, "I lost my great love, but that was my fate, it has nothing to do with you."

Grandmother: I lost my great love, but that was my fate, it has nothing to do with you.

Payne to Patricia: How does that feel now?

Patricia: I feel angry and sad, sad for my grandmother. I'm also sad for my mother, it's sad for all of us.

Payne to Mother: Look at your daughter and say to her, "It was my fate, I couldn't avoid it, I did it for my mother. It has nothing to do with you. Leave it with us."

Mother: (with a mixture of tears and authority towards her daughter) It was my fate, I couldn't avoid it, I did it for my mother. It has nothing to do with you. Leave it with us.

Payne to Patricia: How does that feel now?

Patricia: It feels much better, but I can't bring myself to look at my French fiancé.

Payne takes Patricia's representative and stands her on the left side of her French fiance.

Payne to Patricia: Look at him.

Patricia's representative looks at her French fiance and sobs loudly.

Payne to Patricia: Say to him, "I couldn't avoid it, it was my fate."

Patricia: I couldn't avoid it, it was my fate.

Payne to Patricia: How does that feel?

Patricia: My heart feels broken.

Payne to Patricia: Look at him again and say just that.

Patricia: My heart feels broken (she sobs)… I loved you deeply, I still do.

The representative for the French fiancé embraces Patricia Representative and they both sob together.

Payne to Patricia: Say to him, "It's a pity that things went the way that they did, for I loved you dearly."

Patricia: It's a pity that things went the way that they did, for I loved you dearly.

Payne then takes Patricia's representative and places her in front of her mother and grandmother and asks her to bow before them.

Payne to Patricia: Say the words "Dear Mother and Grandmother, yours was a difficult fate. Respectfully, I leave it with you."

Patricia: Dear Mother and Grandmother, yours was a difficult fate. Respectfully, I leave it with you.

Payne now replaces representative with the client, Patricia herself.

Payne to Client: How does that feel now?

Client: It's very difficult. I feel angry that my grandmother couldn't marry the man she loved. This is difficult to let go of.

Payne to Client: OK, say to both your Grandmother and Mother, "Out of loyalty to you, I will suffer the same fate."

Client: Out of loyalty to you, I will suffer the same fate.

Payne to workshop attendees: You see, she no longer cries, but she smiles, such is her loyalty to her mother and grandmother, she's proud of it.

Payne to Client: So what do we do now?

Client: I don't know. I feel stuck. I want to solve this, but it feels difficult to abandon my grandmother. I think I need a little more time to let this all sink in.

Payne to Client: OK, that's what we'll do, we'll leave it a little while for it all to sink in, then you can decide what your next step is.

Conclusion

The Family System, just like the Soul, seeks balance through including all that which is excluded. As the great-grandparents had forbidden the marriage of their daughter (Patricia's grandmother) to her great love on the grounds of religion, Patricia's grandmother's love became excluded. In order to redress this imbalance, and out of loyalty to her own mother, Patricia's mother likewise denied herself her great love by leaving him prior to marriage. Patricia in turn, not only followed suit out of loyalty to her mother and grandmother, but additionally chose to re-enact this family drama through choosing a French lover, just as her grandmother had done. Family Constellations has an uncanny way of revealing such extraordinary twists of fate.

Although initially surprised by what was revealed in her constellation, when she became fully conscious of the events in the family and the repeating pattern, Patricia had great difficulty in disentangling herself from her grandmother's story, feeling deeply that if she went on to be happy, she would in some way betray her grandmother. Patricia felt a strong bond of loyalty to her grandmother, more so than to her mother. We can conclude that her loyalty to her grandmother was stronger because her own mother had left her fiancé out of free will, even though compelled to do so owing to the entanglement within the family system. It would appear that as her grandmother was forced to separate from her French fiancé owing to religious values, Patricia's loyalty was strong as a result of the great injustice she felt. We worked together a few times over a period of a year, and eventually she was able to release herself from the bondage of loyalty to her grandmother. What is interesting to note here, is that the various representatives we used for her grandmother all responded in a similar fashion, smiling and feeling relieved once her granddaughter let go and could get on with her life. Finally, Patricia decided to go ahead and marry her current fiancé and felt complete with her former French fiancé.

A lesson to learn from this particular constellation set-up is that the Souls of those who have suffered are unhappy when they see others take on or suffer a similar fate out of loyalty to them. Just as our own parents wish us to flourish and be happy, so it is with Souls towards whom we have unbalanced loyalties. For them, the loyalty neither serves them nor improves their situation. Their greatest wish is that others within the family can be free to enjoy all of life's rich blessings.

When a first love is lost

Peter was in his mid-forties when I worked with him. He felt that he had been searching his entire life for his one true love and in the process had had more than 200 female partners. He reported that he either had no feelings whatsoever, engaging his female partners in sex and then moving on, or he fell in love, and the instant that happened, he ended the relationship. On further investigation into Peter's family system, it was revealed that both his maternal and paternal grandfathers had lost their first loves. In both instances the grandfathers' fiancées had died of tuberculosis just months prior to their scheduled weddings. Through setting up constellations for him, it was apparent that neither of his grandfathers could look at their wives (Peter's grandmothers), but looked longingly at their first loves. Peter's entanglement in the fate of his grandfathers led him to take on their feelings, for he too was searching for the lost love. It was as if each time he met a woman, inwardly he would say, "This is not my grandfathers' great love, I'll keep on looking for her." After several constellations, Peter is now able to view a woman from the perspective of an adult, instead of that of a boy looking for a lost dream.

I'm Tearing My Hair Out

Susan is 45 years old and has a small bald patch on the top of her head. She explained that she had been compulsively pulling hairs for as long as she could remember. She also added that she had tried many therapy modalities including hypnosis and regression therapy and over the years had seen many therapists regarding her compulsive behaviour. During the pre-constellation interview, she revealed that her mother had died in a car accident when she was twelve years old, but could not remember if the hair pulling had started prior to her mother's death or after. She stated, "I've been doing this for as long as I remember. I pull at least six to eight hairs out a day, and nothing has helped."

I asked her if anyone had reason to tear their hair out in the family. Her only response was that her father had had an affair and that her parent's marriage was not a happy one.

The client chose representatives for her father, her mother and for herself. The constellation was set up thus:

* Triangle indicates direction representative is facing

Figure 1

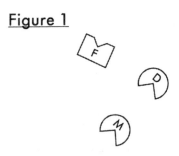

F: Father   D: Daughter   M: Mother

Payne to Father: How are things here?
Father: I want to leave, this is all too much for me.
Payne to Daughter: I notice that you are looking intensely at your mother's back.
Daughter: Yes, I can't take my eyes off her. I feel extremely worried about her, plus I have a sickening feeling in my stomach.

Payne walks over to Mother's representative. He notices that the mother is holding her hands on the sides of her head, as if massaging them rigorously and looking intently down at the ground.

Payne to Mother: How are things here? What are you looking at?

Mother's representative is unable to speak, she shakes her head a little back and forth and starts breathing more erratically. Looking directly at the client.

Payne to Client: Who else died in the family?

The client hesitates a little.

Payne to Client: Your mother is looking at the ground as if looking into the grave, who else died?

Client: My mother gave birth to a baby boy before I was born, it was her first child. He died after three months. It was a 'cot (or crib) death'.

Payne brings in a representative for the dead child, and turns the father around so that he can see what is going on in his family.

Figure 2

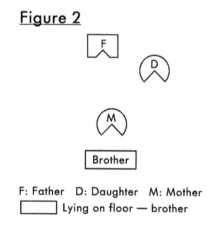

F: Father   D: Daughter   M: Mother
[   ] Lying on floor — brother

Payne places a representative for the infant at the mother's feet. The representative spontaneously curls up into a fetal position. Mother's representative becomes increasingly agitated and starts tugging on her hair whilst her entire body shakes.

Payne to Father: How is it when you see this?
Father: It's too much for me, I can't bear to look at it.
Payne to Daughter: I'm overwhelmed with sadness, I desperately want to help my mother.

Payne turns the mother around to face her husband, placing the infant at her feet once more, so that the father can see.

Figure 3

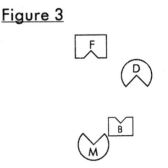

F: Father   D: Daughter   M: Mother
B: Deceased infant brother

Payne to Father: Say to your wife, "I see that our baby boy died."
Father: I can't say that, it's too much for me.

Payne brings in a representative for the paternal grandfather and places him standing behind his son for support.

Figure 4

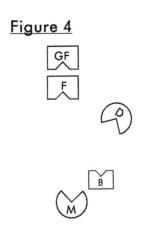

GF: Grandfather   F: Father   D: Daughter
B: Deceased infant brother   M: Mother

Payne to Father: How is that now?
Father: Much better, I can look at my wife now.
Payne to Father: And your son, can you look at him?

Father: With great difficulty, but I can see him now.
Payne to Mother: How is it to look at your husband?
Mother: I'm much calmer now, it feels much better when my husband looks at me.
Payne to Daughter: How are things for you now?
Daughter: Much better than they were, but I still feel agitated.

Payne moves father to stand to the right of his wife and places the infant boy standing directly in front of the parents, facing them. The grandfather is also moved behind the father again, to add support.

Figure 5

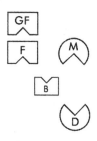

Payne to Father: How are things now?
Father: (sobbing gently) It's very sad.
Mother: It's very sad, but with my husband next to me, it's easier to deal with.

Mother and Father embrace their little boy and sob together.

Payne to Father: Say to your wife, "We mourn together."
Father: We mourn together.

Mother and father look at each other intently whilst embracing their child.

Payne to Daughter: How are things now for you?
Daughter: Still very sad, but I'm not agitated any longer. It's good to see my father next to my mother and I'm happy to see my father holding my baby brother.
Payne to Daughter: Look at your mother and say to her, "Dear Mother, I've carried this out of love for you."
Daughter: Dear Mother (daughter sobs deeply), I've carried this out of love for you.

Payne to Mother: Smile at your daughter and say gently, "Your father and I will carry this, just be my daughter, I'll take care of this."

Mother: Your father and I will carry this, just be my daughter, I'll take care of this.

Payne to Daughter: How does that feel?

Daughter: I feel like a weight has been lifted off my shoulders. I'm still sad, but it feels much, much better.

The representative for the daughter is asked to sit down and the client is brought in to stand in the same place as her representative.

Payne to Client: How does that feel?

Client: It's so sad (she sobs), I'd never given the death of my brother any thought.

Payne to Client: Go and join them and allow this image of your mother and father holding your brother go into your Soul. Feel it in your body.

Susan the client, walks over to her father, mother and baby brother and joins in their embrace.

The constellation ends and Susan the client returns to sit next to Payne.

Payne to Client: How is that now?

Client: I feel overwhelmed and calm at the same time. My mind is racing trying to figure this out.

Payne to Client: That is why I asked you who had reason to 'tear their hair out'. It is a very descriptive expression to describe desperation. People say it all the time, don't they?

Client: Yes, but I had never imagined this scenario.

Payne to Client: Don't try to analyse, it will only get in the way of the healing power of this work. Feel the changes in your body and take the image of your brother, father and mother together in that way. Then we'll see what happens with your hair (smiling).

Conclusion

When a child dies in a family, unless both parents are able to look at the child and see one another's grief fully, the burden of grief for one of the parents becomes too much to bear. In this case, the father could not look at his grieving wife or say the words, "I see that our baby boy died." In this sense, he excluded both his son and his wife. The nature of the Soul is to be inclusive of all things, whether we are talking of the family Soul or the individual Soul. Whatever is excluded will be included in some way. Susan responded to this exclusion in a deep but unconscious way through including her mother's excluded feelings as her own.

In such cases, when another member of the family excludes the death of a child, invariably someone else will step in and represent that event or the dead child itself. In Susan's case, her mother was unsupported by the father and she took on her mother's feelings of wanting to 'tear her hair out' for her. A month later, Susan reported that instead of tearing her hair out several times a day, she had only felt compelled to do it three or four times in the first week after the constellation, twice in the second week and has not returned to her compulsive behaviour since. Several months after this constellation, she reported feeling that she wanted to start plucking a hair from her scalp when she felt under great stress, but now has the self-control not to do so.

I've been sad all of my life, my heart hurts and I don't know why

Jessie was a woman in her mid-forties. She was a successful career woman, had her own business and travelled quite a lot. She was drawn to Family Constellation work as she had been exploring many different alternative healing and therapy modalities and was seeking a solution to her lifelong battle with sadness.

Payne to Jessie, the Client: What would you like to work with?
Client: I've been struggling my whole life with sadness; I just don't know where it comes from. Sometimes the sadness is deep, at other times it's just in the background, but it's always there.
Payne to Client: Has anything happened in your life or in your family to make you sad?
Client: I guess, a few things, but nothing more than other people. My sadness has been with me since childhood. I've tried many avenues of exploration, but I just can't seem to pinpoint it.
Payne to Client: Were there any tragedies in your family? Did your mother lose any children?
Client: No, nothing, everything was normal.

Payne to Client: What about a generation back on both your father's and mother's side of the family?

Client: Nothing that I know of on my father's side of the family. My mother had a brother who was placed in an institution.

Payne to Client: Please tell me about that.

Client: My grandmother gave birth to twin boys who had Down's syndrome. One of the twins died at an early age and the other was placed in an institution.

Payne to Client: Why was he placed in an institution? Was he severely handicapped as well?

Client: It was in the 1950s and doctors told my grandparents that it would be best for the boy to be placed in an institution. He only had Down's syndrome, or was a 'Mongol' as they called it in those days.

Payne to Client: That's very sad, indeed. His twin dies, then your uncle is placed in an institution. Have you ever met him?

Client: No, no one really ever wanted to speak about him. He lived on the other side of the country. He died a little while ago. I never met him (wipes tears from her eyes).

Payne to Client: Would you like to work with this?

Client: Yes, I think it is important.

Payne to Client: What's happening now?

Client: I feel so sad, this is such a sad story, my poor uncle.

Payne instructs Jessie, the client to choose a representative for herself, her mother, her grandmother, grandfather and her two uncles.

Figure 1

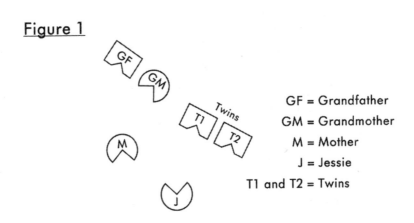

GF = Grandfather

GM = Grandmother

M = Mother

J = Jessie

T1 and T2 = Twins

Payne to Client: What's the first thing you notice with this constellation?

Client: My mother is looking at me, and my representative is the only one looking at the twins.

Payne to Client: That's right. Well, let's see what can be done.

Payne walks into the constellation.

Payne to Mother: How are things here?

Mother: I am very aware of my daughter and I can see the twins out of the corner of my eye, but I'm afraid to look.

Payne to Grandmother: How do you feel here?

Grandmother: I feel a heavy weight on my shoulders and it is a little difficult to breathe. I can also see them out of the corner of my eye, but I can't look.

Payne: Them?

Grandmother: (she hesitates) The twins.

Payne: How does it feel when you say 'the twins'?

Grandmother: Terrible, I can barely say it. It's more difficult to breathe now when I say that.

Payne to Grandfather: How are things with you?

Grandfather: OK.

Payne to Grandfather: OK? I notice that you are looking out in the distance. What are you looking at?

Grandfather: Nothing. I don't want to look at my family.

Payne turns all of the representatives so that they can see the twin boys.

Figure 2

Twins
T1 = Paul
T2 = Peter

Payne to Client: What were the names of the twins?

Client: Peter and Paul.

Payne to Client: Which one died? And who was the oldest?

Client: Paul died, he was the eldest, and Peter lived.

Payne to Peter: How are things with you?

Paul: (representative can barely speak, tears rolling down his face) Lonely, very lonely, very sad, terrible sadness.

Payne to Jessie's Representative: How are things with you?

Jessie's Representative: There's more sadness here than I can hold in my body, it's like being totally alone, my heart hurts, it's a physical pain. I want to do something but feel overwhelmed with sadness.

Payne to Jessie's Mother: How are things with you?

Jessie's Mother: I feel all sorts of things, guilt mostly, but terrible sadness. I keep on wanting to look at my father and mother to see if it is OK that I'm looking at my brother.

Payne takes twins and stands them directly in front of the representatives of Jessie's grandmother and grandfather.

Figure 3

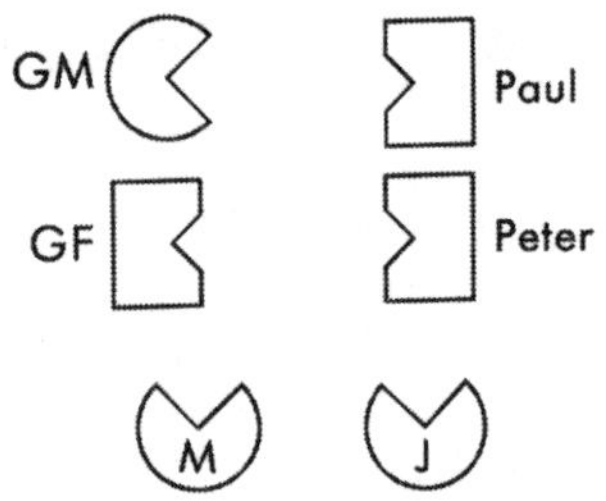

Payne to Grandfather (father of twins): Look at your sons.

Grandfather: I can't (he looks at the floor).

Payne to Grandfather: Please try for me, just lift your head and look at your boys.

Grandfather, father of the twins, lifts his head and sobs loudly. His wife gets closer and they sob together whilst looking at the boys.

Payne to Grandparents: Take Peter, the child who lived and bring him close to you.

Peter resists the movement, he doesn't want to get closer to his parents. Payne suggests that the grandparents take both boys together. Peter relaxes and notices that Paul is smiling.

Payne to Paul: You are smiling, what's happening with you?
Paul: I'm happy for my brother.

Grandparents and the twin boys embrace and sob together, grandfather motions to his daughter, Jessie's mother to join in the embrace, Jessie's representative is left on the outside watching.

Figure 4

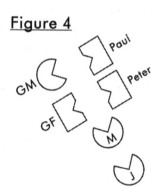

Payne to Jessie's Representative: How is it for you now?
Jessie's Representative: (sobbing) It's such a relief to see them all together.

Payne replaces representative with the client.

Payne to Client: Look at them. How does that feel?
Client: I just want to hug my Uncle Peter.

Payne moves Jessie to stand in front of her uncle Peter.

Figure 5

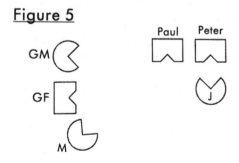

Payne to Client: Say to your uncle, "Beloved Uncle, I've missed you terribly."

Client: (barely able to get the words out) I've missed you terribly.

Payne to Client: Say to him, "Dearest Uncle, I've carried your sadness out of love for you."

Client: (sobbing deeply) Dearest Uncle..., I've... I've... carried this sadness out of love for you. (Jessie flings her arms around uncle Peter's neck and they sob together)... I've missed you so much.

Payne to Client: Now look at your uncle and say, "I take you as my uncle and give you a special place in my heart."

Client: (more composed now) I take you as my uncle and give you a special place in my heart.

Payne to Client: Say the same to your other uncle, Paul.

Client to Paul: I take you as my uncle and give you a special place in my heart.

Payne to Client: Now stand back, look at both of your uncles and say, "Yours was a difficult fate and I now respectfully leave you with my grandparents and mother." Then bow to them.

Client to Uncles: Yours was a difficult fate and I now respectfully leave you with my grandparents and mother (Jessie bows respectfully).

Payne to Client: How do you feel now?

Client: It was a little difficult to say, "I leave you with my grandparents." I had resistance to that, but I knew that it was right so was able to do it. My heart feels full now, no longer a hollow of sadness. I could never imagine that my sadness was connected to this story, and it is such a sad thing that happened.

Payne to Client: What we see in Family Constellations is that those who have been forgotten or cast out of a family will be remembered, perhaps by someone one or more generations later.

Client: It answers so many questions. Along with my sadness, it has felt as if I've been looking for someone or something all of my life.

Payne to Client: And now you have found your uncle. Look at the picture of your two uncles with their parents, your grandparents, and give that a place in your heart, then you'll be free.

Conclusion

This was indeed a story with deep sadness. In this constellation neither the parents of the twins (Jessie's grandparents) nor her mother (the sister of the twins) could look at the twins directly; there was much sadness and guilt as was clearly experienced through the representatives. In such cases we must ask ourselves, if the parents aren't looking at the twins, then who is left to look at them? In this case it was Jessie herself. Even though she had never met them, within the family system, we see clearly that each member of a family is included somehow by someone. In Jessie's case, she was identified with the twin who had lived in the institution. As you can imagine, this Down's syndrome child was not only abandoned by his parents, but he also lost his twin brother, a very difficult fate. Jessie 'remembered' him through carrying his feelings of loneliness and deep sadness. Such was her depth of love and loyalty towards her family system; she was compelled on a very deeper level to represent her uncle.

The solution for Jessie was to bow to her uncle's fate, as difficult as that was. What we do see through the representatives of those who have suffered, is that they, too, feel relieved when members of the family, a generation or two later who are identified with them, are able to let them go. What we see is that it also frees their Soul as the family becomes more harmonious and all members are in their proper place. Jessie mentioned having some resistance to leaving her uncle with her grandparents, but the lesson here is to remember that this is part of the fate and destiny of her grandparents, too, and has nothing to do with her. Such loyalties can be very difficult for us to disentangle ourselves from; however, at some level we have decided that we know better and are more able to determine the fate of others and the correct outcome, and this is our greatest weakness. When faced with such issues, we need to ask ourselves, "Do I want peace or do I want to be right?" When we seek peace and cease placing ourselves above those who came before us, we can truly give each person involved in a family story a place in our heart and reach deeper levels of humility, grace and love as the Orders of Love are restored.

I've been angry all of my life

Robert is 38 years old and reports being angry all of his life. He is South African of Afrikaans descent and his family fought against the British during the Anglo-Boer War. He explains that he often gets into fits of rage and becomes afraid of himself. He tells me that it is having an effect on his marriage.

I asked him if anything had happened in his life that made him so angry.

He stated, "Nothing I can think of, I've always been this way. Since my wife had our children it's been getting worse. She has threatened to divorce me unless I solve this problem."

Payne directs Robert to choose representatives for himself, his mother and his father.

Figure 1

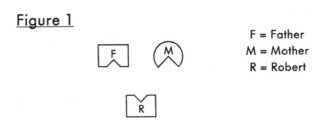

F = Father
M = Mother
R = Robert

Payne to Mother: How are things here?

Mother: I'm shaking inside, I'm so angry!

Payne to Father: So how are things here?

Father: Actually OK, I'm a little puzzled, but nothing much, I'm just standing here.

Payne to Robert's Representative: How are things here?

Robert: I'm fixated on my mother, very curious. Plus my hands are spontaneously making a fist. Almost like I want to kill something.

Payne to Client, Robert: So tell me, what happened in your mother's family?

Client: Nothing as far as I know, I really can't think of anything.

Payne: Well, let's see.

Payne takes representatives for Robert's mother's parents and places them behind the representative for Robert's mother.

Figure 2

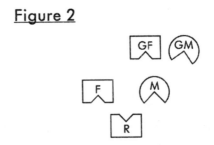

Payne to Grandmother: How are things here?

Grandmother: My hands are clenched and I feel aggressive and very angry. I'm furious, but I don't know what it's about.

Payne to Grandmother: Look at your husband. What happens then?

Grandmother: I calm down.

Payne to Client: So what happened to your grandmother? What could have made her so angry?

Client: I really don't know.

Payne: Your family is Afrikaans?

Client: Yes, they are, all of them.

Payne: What happened in the Boer War?

Client: My grandmother was in a concentration camp when she was a little girl; she was with her mother.

Payne: So what happened?

Client: I know very little, they rarely spoke of it. All I know is that my grandmother had a little brother who died in the camp. He had malnutrition. The British didn't give them enough food.

Payne: You sound angry when you say that.

Payne brings in representatives for the great-grandparents, grandmother's little brother who died, and a representative for the British.

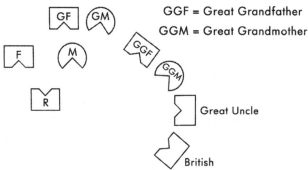

Payne notices that great-grandfather is very agitated.

Payne to Great-Grandfather: What's going on here?

Great-Grandfather: I'm shaking with rage, I feel that I want to kill him (pointing to the British).

Payne to Great-Grandfather: Look at your son, he died at their hands.

Great-Grandfather: I can't look at him. I can only look at the British, I can't keep my eyes off him.

Payne to Great-Grandmother: How are things here?

Great Grandmother: I feel sad and alone. I can see my son, but my husband is far away.

Payne to Robert: How are things with you now?

Robert: My anger became much more intense and focused when you brought in the British.

Payne to Robert: Look directly at the British.

Robert: With pleasure! (he glares at the representative for the British)

Payne to Robert: Say to him, "I'll carry on this war on behalf of my grandfather."

Robert: I'll carry on this war on behalf of my grandfather.

Payne to Robert: I notice that you say that so affirmatively, with confidence.

Robert: Of course, it's my duty.

Payne to Client: How do you feel about what your representative is saying?

Client: Actually proud. It's my duty to hate the British.

Payne to Client: That's an interesting concept. Have you noticed your great-uncle? He looks very lonely and no one can see him. Everyone is looking at the British. So where does he belong?

Payne moves the representative for Robert's great-uncle and places him directly in front of his parents, Robert's great-grandparents.

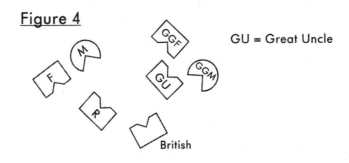

Figure 4

GU = Great Uncle

100

Robert's great-grandparents see their child for the first time and begin to sob. They embrace their child and sob audibly.

Payne to Robert: How does that feel when you look at them like this?
Robert: It's very sad, but I still want to keep an eye on the British.
Payne to Robert: Is it your war? Is there still a war with them?
Robert: No. It belongs to my great-grandfather.
Payne to Robert: That's correct, it's their war, their fate. It doesn't belong to you. Now look at your great-uncle.

Payne turns great-uncle around, with his parents, Robert's great-grandparents, behind him.

Payne to Robert: Look at him and say, "Dear Great-Uncle, it's a pity that you couldn't stay, I give you a place in my heart."
Robert: Dear Great-Uncle, it's a pity that you couldn't stay, I give you a place in my heart. (Robert speaks the words very gently and is visibly moved by what he is saying.)
Payne to Great-Uncle: How does that feel?
Great Uncle: It's a relief! I feel that I belong.
Payne to Robert: Now look at the British once more and say to them, "It is not my war, I respectfully leave you with my Great-Grandparents."
Robert: I can't say that. It's difficult for me.
Payne to Great-Grandfather: Say to your great-grandson, "You're just the little one, this war has nothing to do with you, leave it with us."
Great-Grandfather to Robert: You're just the little one, this war has nothing to do with you, leave it with us.
Payne to Robert: How is that now?
Robert: It's easier now, I feel that I have permission to let it go. (Robert looks at the British once more and repeats the last healing sentence.) It is not my war, I respectfully leave you with my Great-Grandparents. (Robert bows his head to the British and then to his great-uncle and great-grandparents.)
Payne to Robert: How does it feel now?
Robert: It's a relief, the war is over now.

Payne replaces Robert's representative with Robert the client.

Payne to Client: How does it feel to stand here and look at them?
Client: I have mixed feelings. My anger has subsided but I feel some

conflict still. The British have always been seen as the enemy in my family. We even don't like their language being spoken around us; we call it the 'enemy's language'.

Payne to Client: (laughing) So you come to a British therapist to help you with this?

Client: (laughing) Well, that's a twist of fate as well.

(Everyone in the rooms laughs, some laughing as they wipe tears away from their eyes.)

Conclusion

Often, in cases of war—even generations later—individuals can feel compelled to hate the enemy of their ancestors. This gives them a sense of belonging, not only to their family, but also to their social, racial, religious, national or ethnic group. What is once again clear from this constellation is that the dead have feelings concerning these matters. Robert's great-uncle felt excluded and unseen, and felt relieved when the focus of the family shifted away from the British—their sworn enemy—back onto family and those who are included in that family unit. As Robert was clearly representing his great-grandfather's rage, I wondered about his two siblings and enquired after them. Robert explained: My sister married an English-speaking South African, lives in an English-speaking neighbourhood and doesn't even speak Afrikaans with her children. She is a little estranged from us all; it feels likes she refuses to be Afrikaans. My brother is also distant from the family; he's very 'alternative' and feels that he doesn't belong.

As I've not worked with Robert's siblings directly, it would be unwise to give in to too much conjecture. However, it would seem that those who had been cast out, the British and the great-uncle, were being represented by Robert's sister and brother respectively. Once again, we see that the Soul is compelled to include that which has been excluded in order to bring the family back into balance. Once these imbalances have been healed through constellation work, individuals are free to live their own lives, instead of being led by subconscious impulses.

Robert later reported that his anger at home had subsided greatly and that he and his wife had attended some marriage guidance counselling. They have chosen to remain together.

I have a poltergeist in my house

Mary was a divorced woman in her late thirties with an 11-year-old son. She had come to me out of desperation, having tried many different avenues to solve her problem. Mary had engaged the services of psychics, house clearers and shamans in the hope of clearing the very real and terrifying events that were occurring in her home. She had even called in parapsychologists from a local university who had measured the events taking place in her home. She was desperately worried because the activity seemed to be getting more and more violent. It had started when her son was about eight, with lights going on and off, the television turning on and off spontaneously, and various events of that nature. Over the years, the events progressed in magnitude to a stage where she and her son were experiencing violent attacks. Her son had also started to hear voices.

As Mary was afraid and confused I decided not to interview her but to set up a constellation to see what would be revealed. In the constellation we placed representatives for Mary, Mary's ex-husband, Mary's mother and father, her ex-husband's parents, her son Carl, and the poltergeist.

Figure 1

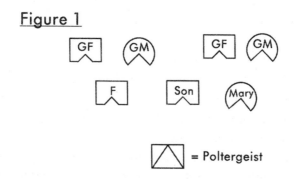

Once everyone was in place, the representatives were asked to look at the poltergeist. Owing to the unusual nature of this constellation, I briefly instructed the other participants of the workshop to centre and calm themselves using their breathing, and to focus on the work being done. I felt that it was necessary to avoid any possible drama or unnecessary fear.

I simply sat, waited, and observed in silence. Within two minutes it was clear to see that the representatives for Mary, her son Carl, and Mary's mother were trembling.

Payne to Grandmother: What's happening here?

Grandmother: Consciously I am very afraid of the poltergeist, but there is something else, I'm in shock... no, trauma... I don't know... but something big happened.

Payne to Mary's Representative: Tell me about your mother.

Mary: Nothing happened in her family that I know of. She left Germany when she was twenty and never went back.

Payne to Mary: She was a child during the war?

Mary: Yes, she was about six when the war started.

Payne to Mary: What happened during the war? Did she see anything terrible?

Mary begins to sob

Mary: Yes, she told me a story just before she died. Their village was just a short distance from a concentration camp. There was an area of the camp perimeter fence where there were some bushes. For several months my mother used to crawl into the bushes and take scraps of bread and bacon to the children in the camp. She felt guilty about taking them bacon, as she knew that they were probably Jewish, but she said the little children ate it anyway. She almost got caught one day, but as her father used to do some work at the camp, they left her alone. One day she took her lunch and some bread in a brown paper bag to the children in the camp at the same place by the fence near the bushes, and the children were not there; she never saw them again. After that, she never wanted to speak to her father and she left Germany as soon as she was old enough and had the money to do so.

Payne to the Poltergeist: How are things with you?

Poltergeist: I'm powerful, I feel very big, and I control all of these people.

Payne brings in two representatives for the Jewish children from the concentration camp and stands them next to the poltergeist.

Figure 2

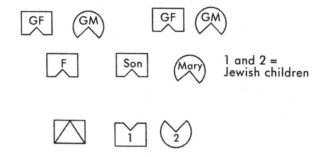

Payne to Poltergeist: How are you now?

Poltergeist: I feel weaker, I feel like a child, like one of them.

Payne to Grandmother: How is that for you when you see the Jewish children?

Grandmother: (sobbing) It's terrible, I can hear a loud scream in my head; I want to scream and scream and scream.

Payne to Grandmother: Then allow yourself to scream.

(It is rare that such things occur in Family Constellations, as the main job of the representatives is to report the feelings that are present so that resolution can be found. However, at times, to allow such expressions of deep emotion can be useful.)

Son: I've got the same scream in my head, and it won't go away. I'm very afraid.

At this point the poltergeist becomes a child and sobs heavily. It eventually falls to its knees, curls up in a fetal position and rocks back and forth crying like a small child. Payne takes both grandmother and mother over to the poltergeist so that they may comfort it.

Payne to Grandmother: Look your daughter in the eyes and say, "This is how I felt inside. I couldn't speak of it, it was terrible."

Grandmother to Daughter: This is how I felt inside. I couldn't speak of it, it was terrible.

The mother and daughter embrace and cry along with the poltergeist.

Payne to Grandmother: Now say to your grandson, "Some terrible things happened when I was a child, but you must leave it with me, for I am the big one."

Grandmother to Grandson: Some terrible things happened when I was a child, but you must leave it with me, for I am the big one.

Grandson looks at his mother.

Mother (Mary): Some terrible things happened when grandma was a child, but you must leave it with her, for she is the big one.

Finally, grandmother, mother, grandson, the two Jewish children and the poltergeist all stood in a group and embraced.

Later, this family reported that the poltergeist activity subsided immediately and stopped altogether within two months of this constellation.

Conclusion

Over the years, I have had several people approach me regarding haunting and poltergeist activity. Most, if not all, have approached psychic healers, parapsychologists, alternative healers and many others, some with success, or limited success, and others have arrived at my workshops feeling desperate. It is important to note that I have found a common thread in all of the hauntings I have ever dealt with:

- A member of the family has been witness to a very traumatic event;
- There has been a murder or multiple murders in the family;
- A member of the family died tragically after being cast out as the 'black sheep', and therefore neither their life nor their death is acknowledged;
- A victim has been denied.

Although all of the above events occur fairly regularly within families, hauntings and other such phenomena seem clearly to be linked to circumstances that either were perverse in nature, or involved great cruelty.

Entities

The Knowing Field is the part of the Universal Energy Field that is around and within everything in the known Universe. Consciousness is energy in much the same way as matter is energy in its most basic form; in fact, many quantum physicists are now telling us that the Universe is simply energy and information.

When we look at trans-generational healing from a purely energetic level, we can conclude that some events create more energy, or have a stronger energetic presence, than other events. In the case of trauma, what can be termed as a 'trauma entity' is created. Often this would appear to become an entity in its own right, normally attached to the individual who had experienced the original trauma; and in some cases, it would appear to attach itself to another individual within the family system. For example, I have worked with young women who are convinced that they have been sexually abused by their father, an uncle or a brother. However, a constellation can sometimes reveal that the experience belongs to their mother, an aunt or a grandmother. In such cases, the feelings are very real. However, in trying to put all the pieces together in order to satisfy the mind, memories are 'constructed' in order to fit the feeling. What is sad about this is that the process is often supported by therapists and often the wrong person gets accused.

Psychiatrists will tell you that Multiple Personality Syndrome occurs when a trauma has been so deep that a part of the individual's consciousness splits off and becomes a separate personality, with its own memories, view points and personality. When this occurs, the function of the consciousness is to form a protective layer, shielding the core of the individual from the trauma. The trauma entity, whilst it cannot be compared to Multiple Personality Syndrome, can in effect become the mask through which we interact with the world. This entity is there to protect us from being hurt; it makes decisions that are safe, keeps us out of harm's way and from perceived danger, and is the inauthentic self that runs our life.

Nathan

Nathan was a young doctor who struggled to make it in the world. He found it difficult to get into a group practice and his own individual practice was not a success. He was still living with his parents. Whilst Nathan was a pleasant person, he seemed very insecure, smiled a lot, and appeared uncomfortable in groups of people—not the confidence we would expect to see with a young doctor. As an individual, he was full of plans, goals, and aspirations, but nothing seemed to work or 'get off the ground'. One day, at a workshop, I suggested we set up a constellation to look at whether he had a trauma entity running his life for him. In the constellation were Nathan's representative, a representative for the original trauma and the trauma entity. What was immediately apparent was that the trauma entity stood right in front of Nathan, blocking his way, and the original trauma was on the other side of the workshop space, quite distant. As the constellation progressed, the trauma entity said, "I'm breathing strangely, very laboured. I feel like a machine, not a person." I asked Nathan if he had been placed in an incubator as a baby. He told me that he was premature and spent six weeks in an incubator as an infant. What was very clear is that Nathan had created a separated self as a result of his traumatic experience, and that it was this separated self, still stuck in the incubator, that was running his life.

This kind of trauma entity was very personal; however, there are other trauma entities that stem from the family system, not from the individual's direct experience.

Raoul

Raoul was a 34-year-old man who was plagued with violent, and what he described as 'perverse', sexual fantasies. He was bi-sexual and found it difficult to form relationships with either men or women. He feared that he would physically hurt them in some way, or that they would discover his secret life of sadomasochism. He explained that his sadomasochistic fantasies started when he was about thirteen or fourteen and he felt compelled to live many of the fantasies out through special clubs and networks of like-minded people in the city in which he lived. He confessed that he was not satisfied by the experiences, nor did he enjoy them, noting that he needed to continuously extend his limitations in order to satisfy the compulsion.

Raoul was from a South American country that had suffered the injustices of a military regime; many individuals had gone missing or had been kept in jail without trial for some time. He explained that both his mother and his uncle, when in their late teens, had been taken to prison by secret police and that during this time both his mother and his uncle were repeatedly tortured, raped and sexually abused. He said that his mother displayed no outward signs of having ever lived through this trauma and appeared to everyone, including himself, to be a normal, loving mother. There were a number of elements to the entire story. Raoul knew of a much younger woman who was kept in a cell next to his mother's, who would scream when she was being tortured. Additionally, his uncle had told him a story about a prison guard who would often whisper, "I'm deeply sorry, my friend, I will tell about this one day. Please forgive me."

When we set up the constellation, it was not clear to whom the trauma entity belonged, but it seemed to belong to everyone concerned with the events that had occurred. We set up representatives for the mother, uncle, two prisons guards involved in the rapes and torture, one prison guard who did nothing and apologised, the unknown woman in the cell next to Raoul's mother, the trauma entity and a representative for Raoul himself. Within moments, the trauma entity moved to stand next to Raoul.

Payne to Raoul's Representative: How is it when the trauma entity stands next to you?

Raoul: I know it well, it feels strangely comfortable, but not comfortable at the same time.

Payne to Trauma Entity: Why did you move next to Raoul?

Trauma Entity: He's the only one who sees me and hears me, I can't go anywhere else.

What eventually transpired from the constellation is that Raoul's mother's cousin was a gay man who had been taken by the authorities and had been held captive for more than a year. During that time he had been tortured and finally succumbed to the injuries sustained during torture and died. As Raoul came from a wealthy, conservative Catholic family, his mother's cousin was never spoken of as he did not suffer for the 'cause' and because he was 'an object of shame for the family'. The trauma entity belonged to Raoul's mother's cousin and Raoul felt compelled to live out his uncle's trauma in the underworld of sadomasochism in order to represent him in the family. Raoul noted that some members of his family who had been imprisoned and tortured during those difficult years had been identified as heroes as a new government was ushered in. However, his mother's cousin had never been mentioned as he had been arrested for 'sins against nature' and was not considered a hero. There was no indication that his mother's cousin was involved in any perverse sexual behaviour, but was simply a gay man who had been persecuted as a result of his sexuality.

Raoul reported that following his constellation his interest in the world of sadomasochistic sex waned gradually over a period of several months until he lost interest in it all together. He was looking forward to exploring his sexuality coupled with intimacy and falling in love.

Gina

Gina was a 26-year-old woman who was deeply troubled by her irrational fear of being abandoned. She reported that she would often be too afraid to sleep at night for fear that when she woke up her boyfriend would have disappeared. She reported that she frequently felt panicky when friends arrived late, or when someone did not return her call. Gina had nightmares that she would visit her parents only to find the house empty of all their possessions and her parents missing. She was frustrated because her obsessive possessiveness had lost her friendships and boyfriends. Through other therapies she had done and our own work together, it was clear that no childhood trauma seemed to be at the root of her deep-seated fears.

When we investigated the family history together, Gina revealed that her maternal great-grandmother had been half black and half white and that her maternal grandmother was one of her children. She told me that her great-grandmother had drowned in a flash flood, together with her son and that her grandmother had survived the ordeal. Additionally, owing to the pressures of South African apartheid, her grandmother was taken to live with a 'coloured' family and never allowed to see her white father again. She also told me that her great-grandmother, together with her son, had been buried with gravestones that only stated their first names, and not the family name of the white father and husband. When we set up the constellation, it was clear that the trauma entity belonged to her grandmother and that Gina was representing her grandmother's feelings.

With such entanglement in the fate of others, clients often find it quite challenging to wrest themselves free owing to the bonds of loyalty. However, what we have observed in almost every instance of such cases, is that the Souls of those we are loyal to in this way are not at rest. When Gina was able to bow with deep respect to her grandmother, the representative for her grandmother smiled, stood up straight and felt strong again. When we carry the burdens of another Soul, not only are we weakened by the misplaced loyalty, but also the Soul to whom we are loyal is weakened. In turn, the Soul is strengthened through carrying its own fate or burdens, whatever those feelings may be. What is very interesting about this work is that clients simply report a feeling and have little to no awareness of where it may come from. However, as soon as the hidden loyalty is revealed through the constellation, most clients display great resistance to giving it up. In addition to providing healing solutions, such constellations provide a window of opportunity in the direction of a far deeper, sacred, spiritual path where we humbly submit to fate...a power that is far greater than ourselves. As human beings, we have been taught to resist all that we don't like; hence the concept of submission to fate is foreign for many of us. There is fear that it will weaken us in some way. On this deeper level of Soul work, it is clear to see that when we cease resisting what cannot be changed, or withdraw our energy from matters that are clearly the business of others, we are strengthened by that inner movement.

A simple question to ask about Gina's situation is the following: Would Gina's grandmother want her to carry this burden? The answer is almost always 'no'. In the rare case when we see that the ancestor is encouraged by another carrying his burden, it simply indicates another problem within the family system which is usually fairly simply solved through more constellation work. In this way, Family Constellation work bridges the gap between psychotherapy and shamanism, for in such constellations the dead are given a voice and resolutions can be found. The nature of the Soul is to evolve and grow; it cannot do so when its burdens are shouldered by others, especially if those others are descendants. In such constellations, both our presumptuousness and dare I say, arrogance, are revealed, for we are often caught in the trap of putting ourselves above those who passed life on to us. When we do so, we are not in the place of receiving within the family hierarchy. See the meditation at the end of this book for further clarity on this.

CHAPTER FIVE

IMAGES OF 9/11

When major acts of terrorism occur, such as the events of September 11th 2001, the individual healing process is challenged and made more difficult by a nation's response towards the perpetrators of such acts. When a national outpouring of emotions such as anger, hatred and revenge occurs, the individuals involved find it more difficult to bring about closure as a cultural imperative arises in which citizens are obliged by the national conscience to harbour specific feelings for the identified enemy. What has been learnt from Family Constellation process is that it is only when the identified perpetrators, or enemies, have been given their proper place, and the overall fate of the individuals involved are accepted and respected, that forgiveness can really take place. When a nation is captivated by media and political rhetoric concerning such events, the survivors who have lost loved ones often take on a sense of guilt when moving though their forgiveness process, for they are trying to move in the opposite direction to the dominant national conscience. This occurs because not only do we belong to our families, but we also belong to national and ethnic groups that form a group conscience. It is often very difficult for individuals to challenge their own national conscience when it is telling them to resist and hate an enemy, when the opposite—acceptance and forgiveness—is in their best interest. Therefore, the healing process in the aftermath of such prominent events can be protracted. At its core, the problem and the solution are identical to that of anyone dealing with the untimely death of an individual, in other words, acceptance of a given fate.

The overall response of those who have lost loved ones is "This can't have happened, it isn't true", or "This should never have happened". Both are normal responses; however, they fly in the face of truth—the hand that fate deals us in such instances cannot be reversed; only our feelings about it can be transformed. Events such as 9/11 are on such a large scale that they have a force and a power of their own which are beyond the control of individuals. There are forces involved, such as nations, ethnic groups, and political interests, that have planted the seeds somewhere in the distant past, where the momentum for such acts of terrorism has often been gathering for years, if not decades. In resisting what is, we are trying to push against a force and power that is far greater than ourselves, and in doing so, we can only lose the battle—which has consequences for ourselves, as well as for our children and generations to come.

Through the representational system of Family Constellations which employs the Knowing or 'informing' Field, we get to experience not only the feelings of the living, but also those of the dead. In this context, and through this healing process, the dead are always with us, as in many shamanic processes. What we see repeatedly is that the dead who have been victims of such acts of terrorism are strengthened when the living bow down in respect to their given destiny. On the contrary, the dead appear weak and bereaved when loved ones who are still alive refuse to accept their fate. The dead are particularly weakened when the living say, "Because you suffered and died so young, I, too, will suffer and not live my life fully". What has been observed in most cases is that the grief of the dead often has more to do with the response of the living rather than with their own untimely death. Each of us, if we asked ourselves the question, "Would my brother want me to live as if I am dead, or would he want me to celebrate the life that I have?" would surely conclude that our dead family member would want us to prosper. Nonetheless, suffering on behalf of others is a common dynamic revealed through Family Constellation work.

I saw them jumping from the building

On the morning of September 11th, Monika, a German woman, was holding her young baby in her arms when the attacks occurred on the World Trade Center. Like many people working in buildings near the WTC, she stood by her office window watching the entire event unfold, the images of people jumping out of windows etched on her mind forever. Whilst such images will not be discarded easily, or ever, what can take place is an acceptance for the fate of those who jumped for their lives.

Payne to Monika: That was a terrible day for you. How would you like to change it?

Monika: I don't know how to change it. I am more worried about my baby. He must have felt the horror that I was feeling. It is still to this day more than I can comprehend, it seems so unreal, and yet too real for me to grasp.

Payne to Monika: Would you like to work with this directly, the ones who jumped?

Monika: I am not sure that I can face them, but I have to do something.

Payne: Well, let's see what happens shall we? We'll include a representative for your baby so you can see for yourself the effect on him.

Payne instructs Monika to select representatives for those people she saw jump out of the building, a representative for herself and one for her infant son.

Monika: I saw a lot of people jump, how many representatives should I take?

Payne: Follow your impulse, as many as you like, simply feel what is right.

Monika takes four representatives for those she saw jumping out of the WTC, two men and two women, one for herself, and one for her infant son.

Figure 1

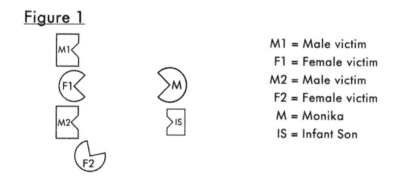

M1 = Male victim
F1 = Female victim
M2 = Male victim
F2 = Female victim
M = Monika
IS = Infant Son

Payne to Infant Son: How are things here with you?

Infant Son: OK. I am a little concerned for my mother, but everything seems OK to me.

Payne to Infant Son: (pointing to WTC victims) And when you look at these people whom your mother saw, does anything change?

Infant Son: Nothing. It hasn't got anything to do with me.

Payne to the Client, Monika: How does it feel to hear that?

Client: Greatly relieved, I was worried about that.

Payne to Infant: Thank you, we don't need you, you can sit down now.

Payne to Monika's Representative: How are things here?

Monika: Terrible. I have a knot in my stomach, I feel sick, lots of feelings, powerless, guilty, angry, sad, everything all at once, it's difficult to breathe whilst standing here looking at them.

Payne: Are you attracted to any one of them in particular?

Monika: Yes, the woman at the end. I feel great sadness when I look at her; I have an attraction to her. I want to help…I'm not sure what it is, but it is like I know her.

Payne to Female Victim 1: How are things with you?

Female Victim 1: I feel restless and also sad.

Payne moves Monika's representative to stand directly in front of Female Victim 1.

Figure 2

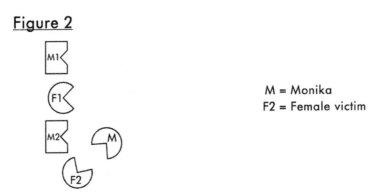

M = Monika
F2 = Female victim

Payne to Monika's Representative: How does it feel when you look at her so closely?

Monika: Overwhelming sadness. There was nothing I could do to help (Monika sobs).

Payne to Female Victim 1: How is it when you look at her?

Female Victim 1: It is strange. I feel sad, but at the same time I am not really here.

Payne to Monika: Say to her, "There was nothing I could do to help."

Monika: There was nothing I could do to help.

Female Victim 1: I know.

Payne to Female Victim 1: Please say to her. "It was my fate, there was nothing anyone could do." (victim has a tear in her eye)

Monika: I don't want to accept that, it's difficult for me.

Payne takes a representative for one of the terrorists without mentioning who he is and silently places him in the constellation.

Figure 3

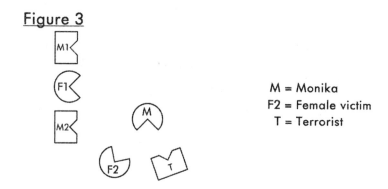

M = Monika
F2 = Female victim
T = Terrorist

Payne to Monika's Representative: Look at this man, how do you feel when he stands there?

Monika: I am angry. I don't want to look at him, I'm really angry.

Payne to Monika: Please just look at him, let's see what happens if you do.

Monika: I am getting even angrier, I just don't want to look at him, and I feel agitated.

Payne takes a representative for a German Nazi without mentioning who he is, and silently places him in the constellation. Payne does this as he wishes to demonstrate the equality of all nations and as Monika is German, this may help her make the shift towards acceptance.

Payne to Monika's Representative: How does it feel when this man steps in?

Monika: Worse, much worse, I can't stand to look at him.

Payne to Monika: Look at the first man, he is a terrorist. Point to the other man and say, "These are my people, we've done similar things."

Monika: These are my people, we've done similar things (she turns to Payne). It's a little better.

Payne to Monika: Do you know who this second man is? He is a Nazi, he belongs to you also.

Payne takes two female representatives from the group and places them next to the terrorist and the Nazi to represent their wives.

Figure 4

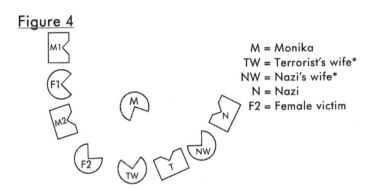

M = Monika
TW = Terrorist's wife*
NW = Nazi's wife*
N = Nazi
F2 = Female victim

* We have no way of knowing if the terrorist literally
had a wife or not. This representation can then be taken
to symbolise his 'family', similarly for the Nazi.

Payne to Monika: Look at these women standing next to the men, how do you feel when you see them?

Monika: Sad, very sad.

Payne to Monika: They are the wives of these men, the wife of a terrorist and a Nazi.

Monika: They suddenly all look human; I can look at these men now. Actually, I feel sad for all of them.

Payne: Now look at the female victim, how is that?

Monika: It feels different, more acceptance, still very sad, but more peaceful.

Payne replaces Monika's representative with the client Monika. He places her to stand in front of all the other representatives.

Payne to Client: You see, they are all human, and they share a common and very difficult fate, that brings equality.

Client: It is very sad. I was angry with you when you brought in the terrorist, and especially when you brought in the Nazi. I've never wanted to look at the history of my country; I've tried so hard not to be German, always ashamed of my heritage.

Payne to Client: Look at them and say, "You all share a common fate, I give each of you a place in my heart." Then bow to them.

Client: You all share a common fate; I give each of you a place in my heart.

Payne to Client: How does that feel?

Client: Lighter, much lighter. I'm sad for all of them, even the terrorist. For the first time he is human, his wife standing there made all the difference. If he has children, my heart goes out to them.

Payne to Client: Look at the first female victim; do you see how she smiles?

Payne to Female Victim 1: How are things for you now?

Female Victim 1: I feel relieved, happy for her, I can go now, and I feel free.

Payne to Client: You see, we don't serve the dead when we hold onto them. There is no right or wrong in this story, it is simply a story of what is, and it can't be changed. The fate that brought all of these people together is far greater than we are as individuals. We have no hope in challenging it and we can only submit to what is. This in turn brings freedom and peace.

Monika moves toward the representatives and embraces each of them including the Nazi and the terrorist. The group is deeply moved.

Conclusion

When such events take place, it is natural that we resist them. However, many of us remain in resistance to that which has already passed, and there is nothing in our power to change it. Resistance is born out of feelings such as, "I was powerless to do anything" or "It should never have happened" and similar sentiments. It takes a lot more energy to resist that which is, than it does to submit to the greater fate that conspired to create such events.

Monika's resolution, or healing, began to unfold when she was able to say to one of the victims, "There was nothing I could do to help." The effect of this healing sentence was to bring Monika's focus to the unchangeable fact that indeed there was nothing she could do. On doing this, feelings of guilt began to subside as she realised that there was no cause for remorse. Without remorse, there is no genuine guilt, only guilt that is based upon an illusion.

Finally, Monika was able to see that the terrorists were human, too, and that there were consequences for them and their families. In that moment she became equal to them, not because her ancestors were German, but because they became human and she was able to embrace them. This movement of being equal to that which we resist, or those whom we resist, frees our Soul from the bond of entanglement; it is a truly humbling experience that is embraced by grace.

My family fell apart after 9/11

Laura is a mother of three. Her husband's brother was a New York fireman who perished in the line of duty at the WTC on September 11.

Laura: My brother-in-law was killed at the World Trade Center on 9/11. He was a fireman. Everything fell apart. My husband went missing for several days; I simply didn't know where he was. Later I found out that he was digging through the rubble to find his brother (sobbing). This went on for weeks. He became obsessed with finding his brother, feeling that he had to be able to call his parents with good news. It broke his heart when he finally had to tell them that there was no hope. His entire character changed and he was no longer the man I married, or the father that he used to be for our children; we were all suffering.

Payne: You are still married?

Laura: Yes, I never stopped loving my husband, although I did consider leaving a couple of times. It was a terrible time for both of us.

Payne: How are things now?

Laura: Things are almost back to normal after three years, but at times I feel anger and resentment. I also feel guilty towards the children because of what they went through. Not only did they lose their uncle, but in many ways they also lost their father, and I'm worried about that.

Payne: You are here with your husband?

Laura: Yes, he is the man sitting next to me.

Payne: Well, let's invite him over.

James, Laura's husband sits next to his wife.

Payne to James: How do you feel about what your wife has said? Do you wish to add anything?

James: Well, she's right, everything fell apart.

Payne to James: Do you wish to work with this directly?

James: Yes, that is why I agreed to join my wife on this workshop. I want things to be better.

Payne to Laura and James: Well, let's begin. Start by choosing representatives for yourselves, your children and your brother who died on 9/11. Decide who will set up the constellation.

Figure 1

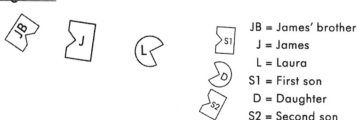

JB = James' brother
J = James
L = Laura
S1 = First son
D = Daughter
S2 = Second son

What is immediately apparent from the setup of this constellation is that James is turned away from his family, looking only at his brother, whilst the mother stands alone looking at the children.

Payne to James: How do you feel when you see this setup? You are not looking at your family at all, only at your brother.

James: Well, that's how it was. It's difficult for me to see this setup, it hurts.

Payne: Well, let's see what transpires.

Payne to First Son: How are things here?

First Son: Not good. I can't see my father at all. I feel a lot of tension.

Payne to Daughter: How is it here?

Daughter: I can see my mother clearly, which is good, but I am also focused on the back of my father's head. I feel a little fear.

Payne to Second Son: How are you?

Second Son: I feel outside in a way, I can see my mother, but my father is away. I feel quite disconnected, a little troubled.

Payne to Laura's Representative: How are you doing?

Laura: It feels very heavy behind me. As long as I can see my children I feel good, but there is a heaviness behind me.

Payne to James: How are you doing?

James: Terrible. I feel like I'm in a fog, but I am also focused on my brother.

Payne to James: Turn and look at your wife for a moment.

James: That's difficult.

Payne to James: Look at your brother and say, "The day you left us was terrible, it's been difficult to let you go."

James: The day you left us… (the representative breaks down and flings his arms around the representative for James's brother. The two men sob loudly in each other's arms).

Payne to Laura: Please turn for a moment and look at your husband with his brother.

Laura's representative almost falls to the floor with grief, then walks over to her husband and brother-in-law and joins in the embrace. The two clients, Laura and James also weep whilst still sitting in their chairs looking at the representatives.

Payne to James and Laura: Did they find his remains? Was there a proper funeral?

James: No, we had a memorial service, we had nothing to bury.

Payne instructs James's brother to lie flat on his back on the ground as if in a grave. He replaces the representatives for James and Laura with the clients and asks them to stand by the grave. The two of them weep and hold one another. The representatives for the children also begin to weep along with their parents.

Payne to Laura and James: Get down on your knees and touch him. Experience that he is in the grave.

This is a very moving scene that touched the entire workshop. After some time, Payne asks the brother, James and Laura to stand and look at one another.

Payne to Brother: Look at your brother and say, "You have a family, dear brother. This is my fate, and they need you."

James: It's true. I've been trying to change this (sobbing), but I can't.

Payne to James: Now say to your brother, "I shall leave you with the dead and go to my wife and children."

James: It's difficult for me to say "I shall leave you with the dead."

Payne to James: Just try to say it, see what happens.

James: I shall leave you with the dead and go to my wife and children.

Payne to Brother: How does it feel when your brother, James, says that to you?

Brother: It feels better.

Payne to Brother: Now say to James, "It was my fate, there was nothing anyone could do, I had to leave."

Brother: It was my fate, there was nothing anyone could do, I had to leave.

Payne: How does that feel?

Brother: It feels true, it's a relief to say it.

James: It's difficult for me to hear, but I know it is right.

Payne rearranges the constellation with James and Laura facing their children, the brother of James next to him, but just slightly further back.

Figure 2

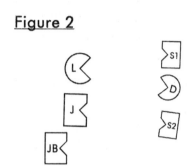

Payne to Children: How are you doing now?

First Son: Much better, I can see my father now. It's also good to see my uncle.

Daughter: I'm happy to see my uncle and especially to see my parents standing together.

Second Son: I feel a part of a family now, not disconnected as before.

Payne to James: Say to your children whilst pointing to your brother, "This is my brother, your uncle. He left us early, but he still belongs to you as your uncle."

James: This is my brother, your uncle. He left us early, but he still belongs to you as your uncle.

Payne to Brother: How are things for you now?

Brother: I feel content and happy; it's good to see them all together now.

The constellation concludes at this point.

Conclusion

Part of the resolution for James was to accept the fact that his brother was with the dead and that nothing he could do would change that. The additional process of creating a funeral scene was chosen, as there had not been any remains for the family to bury. This constellation funeral made the death more real in James's eyes, enabling him to make the next movement of accepting his brother's fate, which in turn freed him to look once more at his wife and three children.

CHAPTER SIX

THE LEGACY OF APARTHEID

There are many questions we need to ask in light of apartheid: How can white South Africans deal with their guilt towards the black community? What is appropriate for white South Africans to do in order to overcome their guilt towards the black community and give them a special place in their hearts? How do the black, coloured and Asian communities deal with the guilt of the white community? What we must become aware of is that all individuals—irrespective of their race—are both participants in and victims of such a regime and system. When white people act out of guilt towards black individuals, they dishonour the inherent strength that the ancestors of the black community possessed in order to endure such hardship. Additionally, when black people view all white people as only guilty, they not only run the risk of becoming perpetrators themselves, but they also dishonour the virtues and strengths of their own ancestors. When we hate a group owing to the suffering of those who came before us, we weaken ourselves. In essence, we label and identify our forefathers as victims instead of acknowledging their fortitude. When we truly honour the fate of our parents and previous generations, we gain strength from them. No longer are they the downtrodden; they become elevated to the status of a proud and strong people who endured against all the odds. With the same posture, it is important for black people to honour the burden of guilt carried by the white community, understanding that forces were at play that were greater than the sum of individuals. Resistance to what is (or was) simply creates focus, and that focus in turn creates perpetuation. When we hold focus on a group and its descendants as perpetrators, we ourselves perpetuate our status, or the status of others, as victims. It is also true to say that in order for there to be perpetrators, there need to be victims; this is the greater dance of fate. So when we truly honour the fate of those who were victims, the power of the perpetrators diminishes, be that real power, or the power we give perpetrators in our consciousness.

When we engage in Soul level work, all are included, no one is excluded, and the visible guilt of the perpetrators is seen and felt with great compassion when both the perpetrators and the victims can grieve together as one. This is love at its highest expression and it releases us from bondage. When perpetrators are excluded from our hearts, we are bound to them and condemned to imitate them in some way. Working through Family Constellations reveals that when a perpetrator is excluded—seen as being less than human or polarised into the position of the 'evil', 'wrong' or 'bad' one— the Soul demands balance and does so by manifesting perpetrator energy within us. When we look around the world, we see that many groups of people who were the victims of regimes, racial hatred and marginalisation by a larger group, manifested within themselves the qualities of their perpetrators. They imitated the actions, thoughts and beliefs of their oppressors, taking the position that they were 'right' and the others were 'wrong', even to the extent of persecuting the 'wrong' in the same way in which they, the 'right', were persecuted. In the same way that the former perpetrators acted in all good conscience, the oppressed rise up and persecute in all good conscience. They feel justified in their actions, and so the cycle goes on and on until the moment we make a movement of the Soul that is inclusive of all Souls, irrespective of the group to whom they belong.

It is the very sense of belonging to a group that can create atrocities, injustice and persecution. As individuals, each of us belongs to a group, be that a family, culture, religion, political group, race or ethnicity. As part of a larger group, many act according to the group movement in all good conscience in order to remain and be counted as a member of that group. It is interesting to observe that individuals who would normally be seen as loving and caring members of society carry out many injustices in the world, including apartheid, in good conscience. So why does this happen? It is the mere fact of being a member of a group that dictates conscience. Each group has its own rules about what is good or bad and each member will comply with those standards in order to remain a part of that group, in order to belong. It is a very rare individual who will risk being cast out of a group by moving in the opposite direction to a collective conscience. It is only when the collective Soul of a group moves to reveal the injustice, that individuals within the group begin to see the deeds of their group in the full light of truth, devoid of the standard that has been set by the clan, tribe, nation or political group. When this happens, all that was carried out in good conscience is experienced from the point of view of natural guilt, a guilt that manifests from within the Soul when any other Soul is not honoured and accepted as an equal.

When we belong to a group, forces that are greater than ourselves are in operation. We are swept along with them and accept almost without question our own group's definition of right and wrong and good and evil. You may conclude that to belong to a group is a bad thing. Groups are neither good nor bad; they are the way in which humanity and individuals define who they are. These individuals are Catholic or Jewish, Zulu or Xhosa, Afrikaans or English, Black, Coloured or White, Indian or Chinese, male or female, gay or straight, left wing or right wing, liberal or conservative. When we belong to a group, we have a need to belong; consciously or unconsciously it defines who we are. We all feel that to be ousted from our group is the worst fate that can befall us. Therefore, we faithfully carry out all the collective edicts of the group—*in all good conscience*—truly believing that our group is right and we are using right use of will. This dynamic lives on deep within the psyche of humanity as the primal experience that survival of our group is dependent upon us defending it from rival groups, or that domination of other groups is essential in order to ensure group survival. This dates back to infant-Soul pre-history. Again, individuals who believe that they are good people carry out much injustice and 'evil' in the world in all good conscience; they are simply carrying out the edict of their particular group.

A movement of the Soul breaks this cycle. The Soul seeks to include everything as equal...actually demands it. So how do we make this movement? We do so by giving a place in our heart to both the victims *and* the perpetrators and seeing all as equal. When we do not do this, there are far-reaching effects which not only influence our own lives, but can also span many, many generations, bringing upon us the same fate of our ancestors or passing that fate on to our children and further generations. Some have come to see this as karma, but in essence, it is the Soul's demand for balance that creates the repetition of history. This works through the process of either identifying with the victims or the perpetrators, or by excluding them from our hearts. For example, if one of our grandparents was a perpetrator of injustice and we exclude him by denying him or his victims, then we, or our children, are often fated to repeat the very same actions, as if driven by some unseen force. In this way, the Soul seeks to make visible within us that which has been forgotten, denied or rejected. In the same way, when there is a denial of the victims of such injustice, we can become fated to suffer the same injustice, the same inequalities and persecution. Again, this is the Soul making visible that which has been denied. This is in no way a 'punishment' or a decision made by any force outside of ourselves, rather it is a movement that springs forth from deep within and one that we cannot resist...the Soul demands equality.

When we experience this dynamic through the method of Family Constellations we see clearly that victims and perpetrators belong to each other in some way. This is a curious phenomenon...one that has been observed many times. The victims and perpetrators belong to each other in the way in which their fate is tied together by a greater force. These greater forces are a mystery, but they can be felt and experienced, and the results of such forces are visible for all to see. When we as individuals—perhaps as descendents of either party—do not accept the greater forces at work and cannot pay obeisance to the fate of other Souls, these Souls, particularly the victims, are agitated and are not at rest. When we engage in a movement of the Soul, bowing deeply with respect to all those involved, grace manifests in the most exquisite way, adding sweetness to the air and a silence that is audible and tangible...for this is the language of the Soul.

For example, when someone dies as a result of a violent crime, most identify with the victim and totally exclude the Soul of the perpetrator. The perpetrator is denied membership to the human race and is excluded on many levels. In such cases, the spouse, child, parent or sibling of a victim who has denied the humanity of the perpetrator and the fate that bound both victim and perpetrator together, is destined to carry the perpetrator's energy within. This may not become apparent until the next generation; a grandchild or great-grandchild can easily pick up the reins and represent the perpetrator, even to the extent of being cast out of the family as the 'black sheep', or simply repeating the same or a similar action. This is a difficult fate for anyone to carry, but it is one that can be dissolved through Family Constellation work.

When we engage in Soul work, it moves beyond blame and honours both the guilty and the innocent at the deepest level. When the fate of the guilty is truly honoured with humility, it loses its power over us. When the fate of the victims is honoured in like manner, their Souls then regain their true power, as if elevated from the position of being the victim, to a position of equality; this can become a source of strength for us. The healing of South Africa lies in our ability to look at the facts of life stripped bare, devoid of denials and pretenses. It lies in our ability to acknowledge what is, without disguise, and our ability to bring that which is hidden into the light of day. It lies in our ability to give each person a place in our heart and to bow to the greater fate of our entire nation that is driven by a force far greater than us, a force which remains a mystery, but is felt nonetheless.

The Black Community

Some of the effects of apartheid and the pass laws that were in place were the difficulties for mixed-race couples, as well as the disintegration and separation of black families. Very often we see that the structure of black family life has been broken down, not only due to the effects of colonialism and the collapse of the tribal system, but also as a result of mothers and fathers working great distances from their family homes. Often the mother worked in domestic service in white suburban homes, and was not able to keep her children with her, while the father worked as a miner, farm labourer or gardener, lacking the financial means to keep his children with him, or even to visit very often. What is tragically visible is that as a result of the loss of culture and tribal structure, many black men have lost a sense of who they are. Having been raised largely by mothers and grandmothers, they often lack the strength and sense of belonging that they would have inherited from their fathers. Similarly, these effects can be observed in Afro-Caribbeans and African-Americans where a systematic separation of men and women took place during the years of enforced slavery, thereby disallowing the formation of natural families. Additionally, with the punitive system that was in place, many of the ancestors of black people were murdered and raped by their captors, with no one being held accountable.

The solution that Family Constellations work can offer black people through the Knowing Field and the use of representatives, is that individuals can once again be connected to their fathers and to their tribal heritage, thereby giving them a source of strength that they can draw upon. When tribal peoples have spiritual, cultural and material poverty thrust upon them as a result of colonialisation and urbanisation, the results are devastating. They no longer have their tribal lands, but have a foreign system of wealth creation placed upon them that has little meaning for their Soul. As they submit to their colonial masters, tribal lands, traditions and means of sustenance are removed, and with this the very core and structure of family life. When we look at indigenous peoples across the world from a systemic point of view, it is little wonder that many struggle with poverty, alcoholism, drug addiction and the ensuing crime. In a very true sense, the poverty and its consequences are the result of spiritual deprivation.

In order for many in the black community to integrate into the new structures of a modern South Africa, two inner movements need to take place. Firstly, a shift in perception of their ancestors as slaves to one of honouring them as a strong people who prevailed against all the odds. And secondly, a recognition of the hidden gifts that both colonialism and apartheid brought. To give an example in the context of Western Europe, the Roman Empire ruled with an iron fist for several hundred years, enslaving the majority in many regions of Europe. The legacy and gifts of the Roman Empire are the languages, culture, religion and architecture of Western Europe. Although brutal in its reign, almost everything that every Western European holds dear as identifying his or her culture is largely Roman in origin, including Christianity. Therefore, for Western Europeans to label and reject the Roman Empire as a bad thing from which no good came would be a denial of who they are today.

Likewise, for black South Africans, it is important to recognise that the imposed European culture will one day become part of what will be considered to be the way of life and set of values that will create a sense of a unique South African identity. When we look at the modern constitution of South Africa, we must honour apartheid as being the father of the New South Africa. Just as in Europe war has been the father of peace, so it is true for the dark days of apartheid. The question must be asked: What kind of constitution would the New South Africa have had if the apartheid regime never existed? Just as some of the darkest days in European history have ushered in an era where there is equality for women, increasing rights for the gay and lesbian communities, rights for children, modern employment laws, a European Union of more than 300 million people with a single currency, so it is true for most countries that have emerged from wars and despotic political regimes.

When we look at fate and the course of history, we see clearly that some of the bleakest periods acted as a prelude and catalyst for massive cultural and social change. Apartheid, in this context, is no different. It behoves us to look at history in terms of its creating who we are today. The struggles of our ancestors have paved the way for us to live in a freer world and we can imagine that, without these struggles, we may not have evolved that much since the age of the caveman. So are wars and regimes always a bad thing? When viewed from the perspective of net results, we have to let history and the fate we have inherited become the judge.

Nelisiwe

Payne to Client: What would you like to work with today?

Nelisiwe, the Client: I am concerned for my family. I come from a mixed marriage, my husband is white and we had great difficulties during the apartheid years. We have three sons and I'm worried for them.

Payne to Client: What is your main concern?

Client: That they find their right way as children who have a black mother and a white father. It was difficult for my husband and me, and I'm worried that it may have been passed on.

Payne to Client: Ok, let's see. Select representatives for yourself, your husband and your three sons.

Figure 1

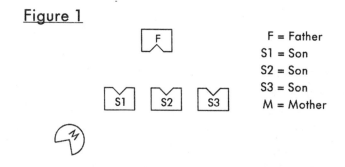

F = Father
S1 = Son
S2 = Son
S3 = Son
M = Mother

Payne to Client: It looks as if you want to leave the family with this configuration, or that you are separate in some way.

Payne to Father: How are things here?

Father: It's good to see my boys, I like having them in front of me.

Payne to Sons: How are you boys doing?

Son 1: I also like looking at my father. I can't see my mother and that disturbs me a little.

Son 2: I am aware that my mother is missing. I'm just a little disturbed by it, but would prefer that she stood with the rest of us in the family.

Son 3: I am very angry at my mother. I can't see her, but I feel very angry at the fact that she's looking in the other direction away from us.

Payne to Nelisiwe's Representative: How are things with you? You appear to be looking at something.

Nelisiwe's Representative: My blood is boiling with anger. I've noticed that my fists are clenched and I feel very aggressive. There's something in front of me.

Without naming it, Payne places a representative for apartheid directly in front of Nelisiwe's representative.

Figure 2

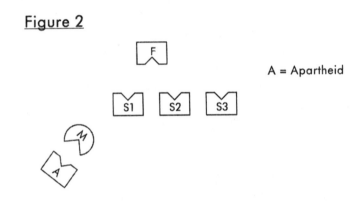

A = Apartheid

Payne to Nelisiwe Representative: How does that feel?

Nelisiwe's Representative: Even worse, my aggression has increased. I want to hit him.

Payne to Apartheid: How do you feel here?

Apartheid: Neutral. She's mildly irritating, but overall a neutral feeling.

Payne to Nelisiwe's Representative: Look at him directly. This is apartheid.

Nelisiwe's Representative: Now I'm even angrier.

Payne to Nelisiwe's Representative: Please turn and look at your family.

Nelisiwe's Representative turns to look at her family.

Nelisiwe's Representative: No, I have to do deal with him first; I can't turn my back on him.

Payne to Client: It seems that you have forsaken your family for the sake of apartheid.

Client: My whole life has been dedicated to healing the wounds of apartheid, this is the work that I do.

Payne to Client: It would seem to me that you gave birth to three boys, not apartheid.

We concluded the constellation without finding a clear resolution. As Nelisiwe was placed next to her husband, her focus remained on apartheid and her three boys remained feeling ignored by their mother. On future visits to workshops, Nelisiwe softened gradually and in time her focus was once again returned to her family. Having witnessed the effects of apartheid on white people through constellation work, she was able to allow her anger to diminish. This constellation highlights that when we get tied up in a cause, or are bound by the events of the past, those who are nearest to us also suffer. For her sons, it was not apartheid that was causing the problem in their family, but their mother's entanglement with it.

Karina

Karina was a professional Afrikaans woman working for what is termed in South Africa a Black Empowerment company. The purpose of such companies is to provide opportunities in career and business to previously disadvantaged black people who have suffered under the apartheid regime. Karina, a white woman of Afrikaans descent, was very passionate about her work until problems began to surface. Here is her story.

Payne to Client: What would you like to work with?

Client: I work for a Black Empowerment company. I truly believe in what the government is trying to do, but I'm in a very difficult position. I work very long hours, sometimes seven days a week, just to keep up with the workload.

Payne to Client: Do you work alone? Why are you working such long hours?

Client: Many of my colleagues simply don't have the skills required for the job and my boss relies heavily on me to get things done. I'm totally exhausted and feel drained; I can't carry on like this.

Payne to Client: Let's see what is really going on, shall we? Select representatives for yourself, your boss, the company and for apartheid.

Figure 1

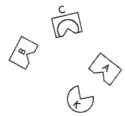

B: Boss   C: Company   A: Apartheid   K: Karina

Payne to Karina's Representative: What is very clear is that your focus is on apartheid, which is in the past. You are not looking at your boss at all, or even at the company.

Karina the Client: I come from a very conservative family; it's a big topic for me. Family members were in the former police force under apartheid.

Payne to Karina: Let's take a closer look. How are things here?

Karina: Heavy. I'm can't look away from him (apartheid).

Payne to Karina: Let's try something. Look at your boss and the company and say, "I'm doing it for apartheid, I must atone."

Karina: I'm doing it for apartheid, I must atone (tears flow down her face).

Payne to Karina: How does that feel?

Karina: I feel burdened by guilt, it's so heavy.

Payne to Client: We need to work with your family. Your ex-husband was in the police as well, wasn't he?

Client: Yes.

Payne places representatives for her former husband, mother and father in the constellation.

Figure 2

H: Ex-husband   A: Apartheid   F: Father   M: Mother
K: Karina   C: Company   B: Boss

134

Payne to Mother, Father and Ex-Husband: How is it to stand like this
with apartheid? Is it your place?

Father: It's OK. This is my place.

Ex-Husband: I'm not comfortable at all, but it is my place.

Mother: I don't really notice apartheid; I'm more concerned for my
daughter.

Payne to Boss: How is it for you to look at apartheid?

Boss: Very angry. I'm agitated.

Payne moves Mother to stand behind Karina's representative as support.

Figure 3

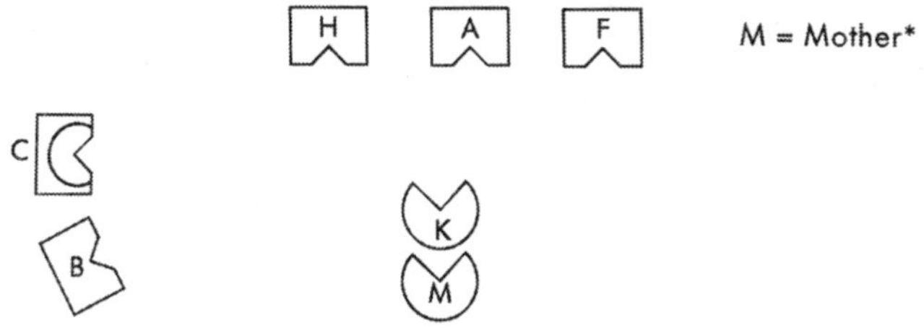

* Mother placed behind Karina for support

Payne to Karina: How does that feel now?

Karina: Better, but still heavy.

Payne: Say to your father and ex-husband, "I respectfully leave apartheid
with you."

Karina's Representative: I respectfully leave apartheid with you.

Payne to Karina: How does that feel now?

Karina: Difficult. I'm a little better, but I can't let go of it.

Payne to Client: What happened during those years?

Client: Both my husband and father were in the police force under the
old government. I can only imagine. In fact, I know bad things
happened, but it's difficult for me to imagine them.

*Payne places representatives for the victims of apartheid next to father and ex-
husband.*

Payne to Karina: Does anything change when I bring these two victims
of apartheid into the constellation?

Karina: My knees are weak. I feel an overwhelming sense of grief and guilt.

Payne replaces Karina's representative with Karina, the client.

Payne to Client: How is this?

Client: It's terrible. I feel so powerless to do anything.

Payne to Client: So your solution is to pay penance for the sins of others by making yourself a slave to this company?

Client: Yes, I've known this for a while. I needed a constellation just to bring it out into the open, so I could see it more clearly. But I've always known.

Payne to Client: We're not quite finished. Say to your father, "Dear Father, no matter the past, you remain my father. I respectfully leave apartheid with you."

Client: Dear Father, no matter the past, you remain my father. I respectfully leave apartheid with you.

Payne to Client: Now say to your ex-husband, "Dear Husband, you remain the father of our children, and together we are the parents. I respectfully leave apartheid with you."

Client: Dear Husband, you remain the father of our children, and together we are the parents. I respectfully leave apartheid with you.

Payne to Client: How does that feel now?

Client: Much better.

Payne to Client: Now turn to your boss and the company and say, "I've been doing it for my father and ex-husband."

Client: (sobbing) I've been doing it for my father and ex-husband.

Conclusion

With such constellations, it appears clear that many white South Africans are struggling with the country's past. This begs several questions. How do white people deal with their own guilt, especially if it is not personal guilt such as Karina's? Likewise, what is the healthiest response for black South Africans to have towards individuals such as Karina who are suffering on behalf of others? Just as when an individual hurts his or her spouse or partner, often the partner will hurt them back in some way, usually to a lesser degree, and this, in a way, creates balance. So it is for post-apartheid South Africa. Affirmative action hurts the white male population the most, either denying them career opportunities or burdening them with extra responsibilities that they must carry on behalf of their black co-workers who often lack the same level of skills. However, skill training has been denied them in the past, so they are not entirely to blame for this current situation. We see a balancing act where the greater hurts of the past are being played out in smaller ways in order to bring about some sense of balance. This is not a comment on whether this is right or wrong, it is simply an observation of what is. We are learning that an 'eye for an eye' mentality eventually creates nations of blind people who can no longer see what they are doing.

What is important is that individuals carry only their own burden of remorse, not that of others. In order for South Africa to be healed, the black population must find a way to embrace the guilt of the white population in their hearts, and white South Africans must learn to take individual responsibility and not to feel responsible for the actions of governments and governmental organisations from the past. When these inner movements are not made, then the cycle of victim and perpetrator simply perpetuates. Karina, for her part, was not doing anything to solve the issue by making herself a virtual slave to the affirmative action system, but was simply deepening her own guilt and playing out the subservient role of black people in the past... and so the cycle continues.

CHAPTER SEVEN

THE HOLOCAUST—
FOR WHOM DO WE MOURN?

When looking at the Holocaust from the perspective of Family Constellations experience, we are posed with the question: For whom do we mourn? Do we mourn for the Jews only?

Traditionally, the Holocaust has been seen as an exclusively Jewish affair, and in some circles, they are the only acknowledged victims. Now that you have read much of this book with many examples of case studies, the answer may be clear to you that the Germans themselves make up a sizeable portion of the forgotten victims of the Holocaust, for the German nation carries the burden of guilt which, in and of itself, results in consequences for today's generation of young Germans. However, together with Poles, Russians, Gypsies, Jehovah's Witnesses, the disabled, conscientious objectors, those of mixed race, the gay community and many others, the Holocaust itself is estimated conservatively to have cost more than fifteen million lives. Additionally, with the additional mass graves found on the Eastern Front, the true figure will never be known. When we look honestly at family systems, we see clearly that there are often serious consequences when victims of injustice are denied or excluded. Therefore, it is great folly on the part of much of the world to have excluded the millions of non-Jews who died in the Holocaust. Today, there is virtually no record or recognition for their passing, despite the fact that the number of non-Jews who died exceeds the number of Jews who perished. There is great danger when one group claims ownership of such mass events; it has the effect of separating that group from the rest of the world, once again giving them the status of a 'chosen people'. History has shown us that 'chosen people' do indeed tend to be chosen for all manner or things, even genocide. Therefore, if we are to successfully break the cycle of anti-Semitism, we need to broaden our definition of the Holocaust to include non-Jews as well as Jews, and view it as a truly European affair, not exclusively a Jewish affair. As Jews embrace their fellow victims, the Poles and others, it will enable them to embrace their fate more easily, and in turn, also see the plight of the Germans, whose history weighs so heavily on their hearts.

During a weekend workshop, a constellation was set up to represent the Holocaust. A few minutes into the session, a Jewish client exclaimed, "Why do you place these people into the constellation, they were not that important" (referring to representatives for Poles and Gypsies). To which I replied, "Are more than three million Poles unimportant?" As the constellation progressed, this client had great difficulty looking at representatives for the Nazis and I gently said to her, "Do you know why you can't look at the Nazis?" "No," she replied. "Because they look to you as you look to the Poles." She was perplexed and said, "I don't know what you mean." "It's quite clear," I replied. "The Nazis don't recognise you as a human being, just as you don't recognise the Poles as having any human importance." I asked her to look at the Poles and bow to them, as sharers in a common fate. Once she had released her exclusivity and ownership of the Holocaust, she could look upon the perpetrators differently, with more equality, clearly being able to sense the enormity of the burden upon their Souls. Through being able to embrace the Poles, she could then embrace the Nazis in a special way, having released her own perception that the tragedy of her people was the only one to have human value.

It is only when victims and perpetrators come together as a result of a movement from their own Soul in order to mourn as one, that the healing of nations can take place. This applies not only to the Holocaust, but also to all human-created tragedies, including wars, political oppression, persecution and genocide. In order to do this successfully, all of the victims need to be given their proper place, with equal recognition, irrespective of whether they were Jews or Gentiles.

Molly

Molly was a middle-aged, first generation American, daughter of parents who had escaped the horrors of the Holocaust in 1938. Both of her parents lost their entire families.

Towards the end of Molly's constellation, there was a deeply touching moment that filled the workshop space with an energy and feeling that I can only describe as grace. The following is a brief snippet that captures the moment:

Figure 1

Molly is standing facing the representative for a Nazi. Beside them several representatives lay on their backs on the floor, representing the Jewish victims of the Holocaust.

Payne to Molly: Look at the Nazi, and make eye contact with him.

Molly: I don't want to.

Payne to Representative for the Nazi: How do you feel?

Nazi: Very heavy, I can't bear to look at them (pointing to the dead on the floor).

Payne to Molly: Perhaps you can see that he is human now?

Molly: I still don't want to look at him.

Payne to Molly: Well, let's see if we can do something. Are you willing?

Molly: It depends, but I guess so.

Payne to Molly: Let's step closer, that's right, stand right in front of him, look him in the eyes and say to him, "I see that your burden of guilt is heavy. I respect the difficult fate you have chosen for yourself."

Molly: I see that your burden of guilt is heavy. I respect the difficult fate you have chosen for yourself.

Payne to Molly: How does that feel now?

Molly: Lighter, I almost feel friendly towards him, but I'm still wary.

Payne gathers representatives to stand in for the Nazi's children and grandchildren, plus another to represent the German Nation.

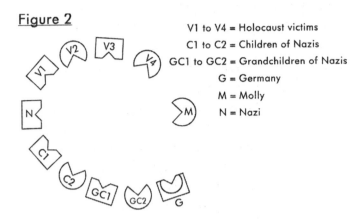

Figure 2

V1 to V4 = Holocaust victims
C1 to C2 = Children of Nazis
GC1 to GC2 = Grandchildren of Nazis
G = Germany
M = Molly
N = Nazi

Payne to Molly: Look at them. Do you have any idea who they are?

Molly: No, but I feel strangely drawn to them in some way.

Payne to Molly: Look at them more closely. They are his children and grandchildren. The one on the end represents Germany itself.

Molly: I feel sad for them. Look how sad they all look (Molly weeps).

Payne to Molly: Now look back at the Nazi, how does he seems to you?

Molly: He looks even more heavily burdened.

Payne to Molly: Say to him, "I see that you are human, too. I mourn for your family as well. We mourn together."

Molly: (in tears) I see that you are human, too. I mourn for your family as well. We mourn together.

Molly embraces the Nazi tenderly and together they weep.

After the constellation Molly adds: I've always denied the Germans, even though I have German colleagues and some friends. I simply shut them out of my heart, not as individuals, but as a people. When I saw it presented like this, saw just how burdened his children and grandchildren were by the terrible things that happened, my heart was rent in two. I never felt that I could forgive the Germans, I've spent a whole lifetime on this subject and I feel free within a matter of minutes.

Payne to Molly: Do you know why you can forgive the Germans now and not before? You suddenly saw them as equals, instead of the 'bad ones'. When forgiveness comes from a place of the 'good' forgiving the 'bad', it never works. Forgiveness comes from equality.

Molly: I never saw it like that before.

Payne: We must mourn for the perpetrators, too, not out of pity, but through the understanding that their burden is also great, and equally so for their children and grandchildren.

In Western culture, forgiveness for such atrocities becomes a great challenge as our Christian-dominated religious doctrines have deeply embedded within our psyche the notions of judgment, hellfire and a punishing God. How then do we overcome this cultural impulse? Although many aspects of Family Constellation work are pure psychotherapeutic process, a great deal of this work enters into the realm of the Soul. Through its representational system, the dead are given a voice. Naturally, this voice in not verifiable; however, as a representation of living individuals is possible, and there is much verification for the thoughts and feelings expressed, we can assume that the dead are likewise accurately represented. When working with the descendents of victims and perpetrators of the Holocaust and other atrocities of similar magnitude, we allow a constellation to flow with minimal or no intervention from the therapist in what Bert Hellinger terms a Movement of the Soul.

Mark

Mark's father had survived the Holocaust by going into hiding in Warsaw. His father was 16 years old when he returned to his home one day and found that his entire family had been taken away. Mark's father had no living relatives... all had perished. After the war, his father managed to escape to Italy where he lived for a short while before immigrating to South Africa.

Payne to Mark: What would you like to work with?

Mark: I am having problems with my fiancée, Linda. We plan to get married but we argue a lot.

Payne to Mark: What do you argue about?

Mark: Lots of things, especially about religion. She's a Christian and I want to raise our children as Jews. I can't do it any other way.

Payne: Well, she's here, let's bring her over.

Payne to Linda: How would you describe the problem?

Linda: It's like I don't have a place. For our children to be raised Jewish, I would need to convert, and even then I feel that I won't be accepted.

Payne: Let's have a look. Choose representatives for yourselves, one for Abraham and one for Christ, and let's see what happens.

The representatives are placed and simply left in silence for several minutes. After a while, Mark's representative stands transfixed by Christ and is visibly shaking. The shaking turns into tears and the representative starts to look and feel very weak, his knees are beginning to bend. Linda's representative stands next to Abraham and simply looks, but is also moved by what she sees.

Payne replaces Mark's representative with the client Mark.

Payne to Client: Simply feel what emerges here.

Mark begins to shake in a similar fashion to his representative and tears begin flowing down his face.

Payne to Client: It seems as if you are afraid of your fiancée's God?
Client: Yes, I'm terrified.
Payne to Client: Continue looking.

Linda's representative crosses the floor and stands next to her God, Jesus, bringing Abraham with her. The three, Linda, Jesus and Abraham stand directly in front of Mark. Payne adds a Jewish victim of the Holocaust to the constellation.

After a few moments, the victim of the Holocaust embraces Mark and he sobs from the depth of his being. The victim smiles at him and gently runs her fingers through his hair. She then gestures towards Christ and smiles. Mark stands before Christ and bows deeply, then stands up straight again, looking directly at Christ. He looks at Linda who is also weeping. Mark then prostrates himself on the floor, fingers touching the feet of Christ. The room is silent. Linda's representative follows suit, lies next to Mark, and prostrates herself at the feet of Abraham and a great peace envelops the room. In silence, Linda the client moves into the constellation and replaces her representative, lying next to Mark face down on the floor at the feet of Christ and Abraham. Linda and Mark reach out to one another and join hands as they lie there in touching silence. The constellation ends.

Payne to Client: It was very clear, you were afraid of her God.
Client: (weeping) Yes, very afraid. So many members of my parent's families were lost in Poland.
Payne to Client: It is interesting to see who helped you. That woman was a representative for one of the dead victims. Do you remember how kindly she looked upon you?
Client: Yes, she made all the difference. I've always felt that I would be betraying my family if I married a Christian, they lost so much.

Payne to Client: And how do you feel now?

Client: At peace.

Payne to Linda: How do you feel now?

Linda: I feel that I can convert for the sake of our children now. I feel safe and acknowledged. When Mark bowed to Christ I felt free and seen for the first time.

Payne to the Representative for the Holocaust Victim: How was the role for you?

Representative: You didn't tell me whom I was representing, but I felt it immediately. I had a sense of great peace and overwhelming love for Mark. I had no problem with either Christ or Abraham. It was a wonderful experience. Thank you.

This Movement of the Soul revealed Mark's deep-seated fear of Christians and their God and the feeling that he would be betraying his family by marrying a Christian. Through this Movement of the Soul, the dead were given a voice and a place, and it was from the dead victim that Mark gained both strength and solace.

Petra

Petra had been suffering from depression for many years. She outwardly stated that she hated being German and emigrated as soon as she was old enough.

Payne to Petra the Client: What happened in the war with your family?

Client: I don't know, no one wants to talk about it.

Payne to Client: And how do you feel about it?

Client: Ashamed. The fact that there are Jews on this workshop today gives me the feeling of wanting to hide. My accent is so German, it makes me so visible and I hate that.

Payne to Client: Well, let's see what we can do. Please select three representatives for German perpetrators, three representatives for Jewish victims, plus one for yourself.

Petra places the representatives facing herself, and her representative between the two rows at the end of the line.

Figure 1

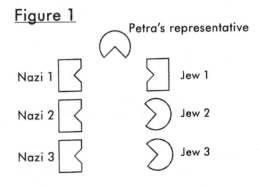

The representatives are asked to stand in silence and simply to follow their inner impulses as they emerge. After a couple of minutes, all three victims have tears running down their faces and one of the perpetrators hangs his head low and sobs loudly, unable to console himself. Another perpetrator turns away to face the opposite direction, whilst the third perpetrator begins to shake from head to toe. Petra's representative clutches her stomach and falls to her knees, also sobbing. After a little while, one of the victims crosses the floor and comforts the perpetrator who is sobbing loudly. He gently caresses the perpetrator and the perpetrator utters, "I don't deserve this kindness," and the victim comforts him as a mother might comfort a wounded child. The scene is very touching. A few moments later, the other two victims of the Holocaust cross the floor to Petra's representative and help her up into a standing position, then hold her from behind. A little while later, the Holocaust victim who is comforting one of the perpetrators brings him over to stand in front of Petra's representative. He places one hand on the perpetrator's

Figure 2

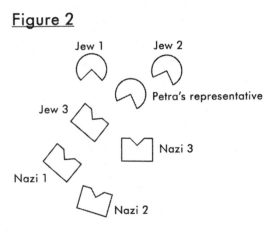

shoulder and the other on Petra's representative's shoulder and smiles. The perpetrator and Petra's representative weep as they first look at one another, and then embrace. The victims all smile whilst they, too, weep.

Payne to Client: How do you feel now?
Client: I feel relieved, like I'm forgiven. I feel that I can now look
Germans and Jews in the eye and feel OK about it.

Petra looks around the room and makes eye contact with the Jews present in the workshop. She spontaneously gets up, walks over to them and hugs them. After a few moments, she realises that there is another German on the workshop and invites her to join in the group hug. It is a very touching scene.

This inner Movement of the Soul is about being able to take our leave of both victims and perpetrators in a healthy way and wish them a fond farewell. As monumental as the Holocaust was, it is part of fate, a fact that is not changeable and one that was created by forces much greater than the individuals concerned. When we consider the greater forces involved in the creation of such fates, we are not talking of external forces, but the internal forces of the human psyche that create waves of change. When we look at recent history, it is clear that such events ushered in periods of monumental social change that were often for the better. For example, had WWII and the Holocaust not happened, would the European Union exist? Although we cannot say for certain, we can suppose that the sweeping social changes that occurred in Europe immediately after the war, laid the foundation for economic, cultural and social unity. It is as if the Souls of both the victims and the perpetrators conspired together to herald in a new era of peace and reconciliation in Europe, in much the same way that the atrocities of South African apartheid have heralded in a new South Africa based on a constitution that is socially ahead of not only its neighbours, but also many other countries in the world, including the United States.

When we look at Hitler and the Nazis from the perspective of the Soul, we cannot help but have respect and compassion for the burden of guilt that they have brought upon themselves. Likewise, when we look at the Jews, we see a people who, for the most part, went quietly towards their death. How do we as either Jew or Christian accept the fate of so many?

When a child is born, it is born into a family to particular parents, into a culture, a religion and a nation; it has no control of this… it simply is. This is fate, and fate is neutral. Fate has no face, it has no opinion, it has no desires…it simply is. So when we are the son or daughter of Jews, born to a Jewish family who has lost many family members, it is our fate, and it is unchangeable. Neither is it desirable to change that fate nor to even want to change that fate. For when we do, we attempt to resist something that, for the most part, cannot be fathomed, and is much greater than ourselves. It is the same for Christians who must deal with their guilt towards the Jews. The movement of fate—large or small—is what shapes nations, cultures and families; it makes us who we are today. When we challenge fate, we challenge the very essence of who we are, what we have become, and what our future potential might be. For fate lends us opportunities for development of the human spirit and greater human potential. When we turn our back on fate, we turn away from the Soul, and deny ourselves the gifts inherent in any movement that we may allow our Soul to make within us. A teacher once said to me, "If you have a question, the answer is always love." I have found this to be true of the Holocaust and many other aspects of fate I have witnessed through engaging in Family Constellation work. What fate deals us is an opportunity to love beyond our human expectation of what love might be. If fate does have a face, it would surely be the face of grace.

Chapter Eight

HONOURING THE AFRICAN SLAVES

During a workshop taking place in the Caribbean, a black woman came forth to set up a constellation. She had done some work before and this time she wanted to work further with the subject of finding her place in the world. I asked if she could not find her place in the world, then where was she? Family Constellations have revealed that those who cannot seem to find their proper place in the world are elsewhere, mostly not conscious of it at all, but elsewhere nonetheless. We decided to keep it simple and choose a representative for herself and also her Soul.

As she placed the two representatives, it became immediately clear that at the core of her being she was occupied elsewhere, not in the here and now. On looking at the representative for her Soul, I was moved to see that her Soul wept and was in deep sadness, looking downward towards the ground. Her representative, on the other hand, looked away from the Soul and upwards towards the ceiling, as if looking for answers from above.

It was apparent that the wound being displayed by her Soul was ancestral in nature and did not originate from events taking place in her immediate family. Based on this insight, four or five representatives were asked to lie flat on their backs on the floor, eyes closed. The weeping continued and as our subject looked at the ones who were lying down, she also began to weep, overwhelmed by a deep sense of sadness. I asked if she knew who they were. She said no, but she felt that she did in some strange way, and was overwhelmed with grief. I gently said to her, "They're on a slave ship, being brought to the new world." Her deep sense of grief grew and her Soul wept profusely. At this point, I also brought in a representative for the ship's captain and the slave owners. Contrary to what we might expect, her Soul became more peaceful, even feeling comforted by the presence of the slave masters.

Eventually through the introduction of healing sentences, our subject was able not only to give a place in her heart to her slave ancestors, but also to the slave master. At last, she was at peace, able to see her Soul and look at the world directly. At a deep level she had felt that it would be a betrayal to accept the destiny of her ancestors, feeling that loyalty to them forced her to reject everyone involved. In this way, she also rejected her own life, for her life as an Afro-Caribbean exists because of slavery: they survived to give her that life.

Many people struggle— as with any of history's darkest moments—to see the enslavement of Africans by Europeans and others in a positive light. So what positive things can be found within this chapter of human misery and despair?

So many African-Americans, Caribbeans, British, South Africans and Dutch citizens of African or Asian origin find little or no strength in the knowledge of the lot and destiny of their ancestors. For many, their heritage seems to be one of despair, discrimination, maltreatment and one lacking in freedom and equality with their white enslavers, who are now their neighbours, colleagues and friends. This chapter is not about racism either then or now, it is about a perspective that can be experienced within the context and life of a family constellation. In Family Constellations, we do not speak of theory or ideas, we speak of observation. Owing to the inherent life of a constellation, active observation can be made of the effect and impact of both historical events and events that occur within a family system, created by family system members in former generations. Many refer to Family Constellations as trans-generational healing.

Slavery, just like other human tragedies including the Holocaust, South African apartheid, the Boer War, the Jewish Pogroms, the Japanese camps in the Far East, the Trail of Tears, wars and other events that influence masses of people, has far reaching effects which can span many generations…at least seven as far as I have observed.

What of the slaves, and how does that heritage directly affect black people today? Before I fully answer this question, I would like to talk about grace…perhaps some would be more comfortable with the word dignity. There can be much dignity in suffering. I do not mean to suggest that suffering is a high ideal, for it is not a condition that many seek willingly; it is something that happens and is imposed upon us. From my observation of setting up many family constellations for people of African origin who are descendents of African slaves, there is great resistance in seeing the plight of their forefathers as anything other than suffering. However, the family constellation always reveals that at the moment a descendant of a slave honours the suffering of his ancestor, the family dynamic changes immediately.

When the destiny of another is not honoured—when their suffering is not held in respect—then the natural flow of love, the Order of Love, is distorted and interrupted. It means that all of the gifts and strengths of the ancestors cannot be passed on freely, for the system is blocked in entanglement. It is blocked by those who can only see the suffering and the injustice. So many are so focused on, indeed even consumed by, the injustice and suffering, that they dishonour all that was good with their ancestors and disempower themselves with that view in the process. The view, in and of itself, becomes a heavy burden which furthers the suffering of future generations, once again disintegrating family ties and laying waste to a culture.

In so many African-American homes the father has not been present. Why is that? Again, I offer not opinions, but observation as revealed by the Family Constellation system that comes to life as we observe it. So many African-American men feel burdened by the plight of their ancestors. Inwardly, so many were stripped of their manhood, their power and their dignity, just as their ancestors were. The remedy to this is to honour the suffering of their forefathers. When suffering is dishonoured, the natural flow of positive energy from one generation to the next is interrupted; it means that the fate of the descendants will reflect the fate of the ancestor. It may not do that in terms of actual circumstances, but other conditions will create the same feelings. In many constellations involving individuals descended from slaves, where the father has not been present in the family, I have the father say to his son (or daughter), "I'm sorry, the burden of our people has been too great, I could not carry it all." It is very clear to me from observation, that the burden of slavery has made it very difficult for many black men to fulfil the role of fatherhood until they honour the destiny of their forefathers.

So where is the honour in their ancestors? In a family constellation, which is a representational system, I have often asked an individual to represent a slave ancestor, although we do not know specifically who that is, or how many there were. The introduction of the slave ancestor into the system reveals much in an instant. The representatives of current descendants often report feeling nausea, weakness and many other physical symptoms; many cannot even lift their heads to look their ancestors in the eye. This response of the descendants, shows very clearly that the suffering of their ancestors has not been honoured and given its rightful place. Had they done so, they would not be carrying the burden for them in this way. To break the cycle of suffering, I ask the slave to say to his descendants, "We are a strong people, and we have prevailed." Or, "We have endured great suffering and yet we gave you life. Because of our endurance, you live!"

These words alone have an enormous impact on those who hear it. Instead of being the descendants of slaves, they are now the benefactors of a people who are hardy and strong, people who have prevailed against all the odds, people who did not give up, people who did not crawl into a corner to die, but people who survived, brought children into the world, a strong people who would not give up! This is their inheritance, and what an inheritance it is!

This small, but huge shift in perspective changes one forever, changes the way in which you look at yourself, the world and your relationship to it. "Wow, how rich I am!" "Goodness, how lucky I am to have been born black! What did I do to deserve such honour and such a rich inheritance?" This is the true legacy of black people in America and in the Caribbean today, not the legacy that has been taught them. Yes, slavery happened, yes, Europeans are responsible for crimes against the black race, but by far the greatest generational damage is done by those who cannot pay obeisance to their ancestors.

In a constellation, the moment that the descendents honour the suffering of their slave ancestors and at the same time honour their strength, the slave feels better, much, much better. The dead never leave us and our ancestors are with us all of the time. Even in death, healing can take place when all are honoured and held in our hearts.

The descendants of African-Americans, Caribbeans and South Africans who were enslaved by apartheid are not so much the descendants of slaves as they are the descendants of a strong people who prevailed against all the odds. There is much dignity and grace in that, and I encourage all people of African origin to bow to their ancestors in honour of what they inherited. The same encouragement goes to Jews and to any group of people who have suffered at the hands of others. It is equally important for the descendants of the enslavers to know that they, too, may be living with the results of ill-gotten gain, guilt. It is very important to honour what is.

Chapter Nine

A PASSAGE TO INDIA

Whilst in the process of writing this book, I was privileged to travel to Hyderabad, India and work with some very courageous individuals in that bustling metropolis. At first, I found India quite overwhelming, just so many people, so many sounds and smells to which I was not accustomed compared to the relative quiet of the wide-open spaces of South Africa. For the first time in my life, I found myself immersed in a culture where I was definitely the odd one out. It truly was a case of East meets West, and this particular pearly white Westerner was the only person wearing shorts on the hot and dusty streets of polluted Hyderabad, much to the amusement of many of the local inhabitants who simply couldn't resist staring at me and observing my every move, however insignificant.

Throughout my life, my mode of learning has been observation coupled with an insatiable need to ask everyone I meet endless questions about their country, culture, customs, belief systems and what makes them tick. As India was so very different, I pondered whether what I had come to know and trust—the age old Orders of Love—would be valid in such a vastly different culture. I wondered if perhaps my way of thinking and what I had observed only applied to Western cultures of European origin. I became acutely aware that despite having given well over 100 workshops, in this country, perhaps all that experience would be largely irrelevant and that I would probably end up offending someone, or indeed everyone, during the course of my upcoming workshop.

For many of us in the West, India is looked upon as being the mother of spirituality. Many of our modern spiritual values have their origins in the 1960s when the Beatles and others brought the ideas and teachings of various gurus to large audiences through music or direct teaching. Over the past thirty or so years, yoga has become commonplace; almost everyone knows what 'Om' means. Much Eastern spiritual practice has become an integral part of Western popular culture, including vegetarianism, Ayurvedic medicine, the state of our chakras, and karma. In fact, in certain circles, if you don't have a copy of Swami Yogananda's *Autobiography of a Yogi* on your bookshelf and have never heard of Osho or Sai Baba, then you are definitely not 'spiritual'. The spirituality of India has become such a vogue in Western culture, that many individuals who were once known as Steve or Jenny, now go by names such as Viyom or Prem after having visited an Ashram in the cradle of spirituality, India. What is this about?

In the West, Christianity has been vilified, often for good reason. We look at the crimes of various churches, the pain caused by hypocrisy, discrimination against women, the unmarried, the gay and lesbian community and we conclude that Christianity has nothing to offer us and hold Indian spirituality up as being superior, closer to the notion of a loving God. Is this really true? After spending eight days in India and getting to know people in very intimate ways through Family Constellation work, the answer is a definite 'no'. It would seem that dogma of Western Christianity is equally mirrored in the dogma of Eastern philosophy. Just prior to leaving for India, a Christian fundamentalist shared with me that the recent tsunami of December 2004 was an act of God to punish the non-Christian nations of Sri Lanka, Indonesia and India for not accepting God's only Son, Christ, as their saviour. Similarly, I heard a report that an Islamic imam said that Allah had punished these nations for the debauchery of Christmas and for allowing a thriving sex industry to entertain Western tourists. This made me curious to learn the Indian view; surely it would be quite different. In essence, it was not. This time it was karma that destroyed the lives of the largely fishing populations in order to pay back their debt to the oceans for all the fish lives they had exploited. It was in that moment that I realised that the need to create a punishing God who would discipline non-believers, was a global issue—not a Christian issue, an Islamic issue, or a Hindu issue—simply a global human issue.

Each of us, at one time or another, while searching for something greater, feels the need to have a prescriptive, defined plan towards unity with our God handed to us by some 'higher authority', who we have somehow mysteriously decided has God's ear and knows God's will. This can be a priest, a pope, an imam, a rabbi or guru. However, is what they say really true? Can we prove it? I don't believe we can. We do this as it makes us feel safe if we keep to a narrowly defined path—no matter how ridiculous or lacking in compassion and understanding for our fellow humans; we are safe, even to the extent of feeling we are guaranteed a place in paradise after our physical demise, or at least a better hand in karma will be dealt for the future, whether in this life or the next. My question is, where is the love? Where does the power of love between humans come into this greater, supposedly spiritual plan? I conclude that love doesn't really come into consideration at all, whether we are Christian, Hindu, Muslim, Metaphysical or New Age in spiritual expression. What seems to be more important is the following of rules and superstitions irrespective of the human consequence, many falling foul to spiritual glamour, having the notion that to be spiritual makes us in some way special or slightly more important than the person next to us. We do all this, sacrificing our humanity along the way, out of a need to belong. We belong to a group, to a religion or to a particular God, whether that God be Shiva, Jesus, Allah or the Buddha. In India, just as in any nation—irrespective of race or creed—when we don't belong to our mother and father, or to our families, we simply don't belong, no matter how many mantras we chant, how often we attend mass, *schul* or evening prayers in a mosque.

The individuals I worked with in India were groundbreaking pioneers and I asked a lot of them. I asked them to bare their Soul, to risk losing face in a society and culture that seems to prize keeping up appearances and obeying the rules above all else. This was going to be a tough nut to crack, and here I was, a white man who ate meat, enjoyed a cigarette during the breaks, and on top of all that, was quite openly gay. Surely I would be forgiven for thinking that I had been caught up in some divine comedy and that the joke was on all of us. Or maybe, just maybe, it was an opportunity for us all to learn that the power of love was the same everywhere. Love knew no race, creed, gender, caste or sexual orientation…it simply was and needed to be acknowledged in order for any healing to take place. My host had warned me that if the participants gathered for this workshop knew that I was gay, some may be offended enough to even leave the workshop. This was not going to prevent me from doing what I love and doing what I do best, revealing the Orders of Love. I wasn't about to remain in the closet in order to appeal to outdated spiritual and cultural values. Not being true to myself simply means not being true. We have a snowball's chance in hell of getting close to God (Love) if it means putting on a good face or pretending to be what we're not.

So let us now look at the systemic problems facing Indian culture.

Interruptions to the Orders of Love

As in other cultures, there are certain events that take place in families in India which cause interruptions to the natural flow of love from parents to children within a family system. The following are common problems in India that have shown themselves to have a deep residual impact, spreading over many generations:

Adoption: It appears to be quite common practice for infants and children to be given away to other family members, sometimes distant relatives, when a couple feels that they have too many children, or perhaps, too many girls. These adoptions are often agreed to prior to birth, sometimes prior to pregnancy, and can either be motivated by giving a child to a woman who cannot conceive or as part of a family business deal where property and money can be exchanged for the life of the child.

Domestic Violence: It seems to be quite commonplace for married men to rule their home with an iron fist, and it is often considered normal and acceptable that a husband hit his wife and children.

Arranged Marriages: Whilst many of these marriages work well being supported by an extended family, it was quite clear from many constellations that one or both married partners had feelings for someone else but that parental approval had not been given for this other partnership. This leaves many individuals feeling trapped in relationships that are bereft of love, both parties feeling that they have no choice but to stay with one another out of cultural obligation.

Widows: They are considered the 'black sheep' of the family. I learnt that in many sectors of Indian culture, mostly in the past, but still existing in the present, widows are considered bad luck. Owing to this, they are not invited to weddings, funerals and other family and religious holidays. This often means the widow has no say in the upbringing of her own children and is often a virtual prisoner within her own family.

Infant Mortality: The instance of infant mortality and abortion in Indian culture is higher than I had experienced in the West, with the same consequences to the family system, often on a grander scale.

The Indian Constellations

The individuals I worked with were all rule-breakers in their own way, bringing out into the open stories, memories and feelings that had been repressed for many years, sometimes for generations. For them to reveal in public their stories of adoption, rape, incest, or their love for another—although married through arrangement—was groundbreaking and daring for their culture.

So were the Indian constellations so very different? In some ways they were, but in most ways, not at all. The main difference was the notable suppression of feelings plus some slight nuances of difference when using healing sentences. The healing sentences that came to life were often culturally specific, which had a greater impact on the resolution.

Arranged Marriage

During one constellation, it was quite clear that the husband was involved elsewhere. The client revealed that her husband was in love with another woman but that his parents didn't approve of his choice and he was forced to marry my client as a result of an arranged marriage.

During the constellation, I had a representative for my client's husband's first love stand to his right, whilst my client stood to his left. Her husband's representative at first 'glowed' with great affection for his first love, and then reported deep feelings of sadness. Within the context of Indian culture, the healing sentence that brought about resolution was, "It's a great pity that things went the way that they did, for I loved you very much. I now give you a place in my heart. Now, in honour of the traditions of our ancestors, I turn to my wife and children for this is my destiny."

This healing sentence would not necessarily work in a similar situation in Western culture. However, as the nature of the Soul is to submit to fate, it was the acknowledgement of the love, family tradition and fate that created a greater flow between husband and wife. When fate is accepted, love can flow; when we resist it, love becomes distorted and aberrations appear; in the case of this family, violence manifested between husband and wife. Another healing sentence that assisted in bringing about resolution was, "When I hit you, love is destroyed, and I am deeply sorry for that. I carry the consequences of my actions in my heart."

Domestic Violence

One man wanted to look at his current family as he felt that he was closer to his daughter than his son, which troubled him. What was revealed was that this man's father had ruled the home with an iron fist and this man often witnessed his father's violence towards his mother. Through the representatives we could clearly see and feel that this had been a pattern for numerous generations, each man—his father, grandfather, and so on—expressing violence towards spouse and children as a way to 'rule' his home. A healing sentence that began the thawing process across generations was, "Real men are gentle with their sons." The client in question cried the deep tears of a little boy as he faced the representative for his own father. After he embraced his own father and called out "Papa" from the deepest part of his being, he was able to face his son, embracing him and feeling safe to be his father. Until this point, he resisted his own son out of fear of passing on the family tradition of violence between fathers and sons to his own dear boy. This constellation was deeply touching for all who were present as it rang true for so many Indian families.

While acknowledging the tradition of ancestors in India contributed to the healing of individuals and families, the overall lesson to be learned was that the truth of love and the inclusion of all was a power far more important than keeping up appearances. Whilst these problems are also present in the West, for India, the return to love is a far greater journey that requires more courage than is usually required elsewhere. For Indian men and women to reveal their true feelings, family secrets and crimes against the Soul, takes a great deal of courage and willingness to move against the flow in their return to love. When faced with such a highly structured culture, the forgiveness movement of being 'equal to' is quite a foreign concept. How can we forgive when we are either inferior to or superior to someone? It is quite an impossibility. In this sense, being 'equal to' means being equal to the pain that has been caused by others through experiencing firsthand the burden that perpetrators carry in their hearts, either through observation or in the role of representative.

India inspired me through knowing, seeing, feeling and touching the spirit of humanity that is alive in all people, irrespective of culture or creed, and that when faced with the truth of love, individuals are willing to take a blind leap of faith, risk losing face, and embrace truth without pretences or masks. Each of the individuals I worked with in India had the heart of a lion, perhaps Aslan, the lion of C.S.Lewis.

CHAPTER TEN

GRATITUDE AND AUTHENTICITY

So many of us fall into the trap of blaming our parents for all of our misfortune. The great impediment to leading a magical life is our refusal to accept what is—simply said, resistance. We build up stories that become fact for us and it is these 'facts' that then go on to become the script from which we sculpt our lives; whether it is within our career, personal relationships or finances, we live life according to this script. Perhaps we are convinced that our mother did not love us enough, or that our eldest sister, or youngest brother was the family favourite. We may bemoan the fact that our father is an alcoholic, our mother is this or that, and then blame much of what has gone wrong in our lives on it. Perhaps our wounds are deeper and they involve physical violence or sexual abuse in one form or another. Irrespective of the circumstance within our family, we can choose at any moment to simply say: It happened, it isn't happening now, and the only thing I need to know is that I have been given the gift of life.

As we are not time travellers, none of us is able to go back and rewrite the events of the past, although many of us live in the past, constantly reliving and regurgitating past events. However, we do have the power to go back and rewrite our feelings and perceptions by looking at what truly is, devoid of the illusions we have created. The greatest obstacle that we have in this endeavour is to fear the love we feel for those who gave us life. We fear this love because it runs so deep—it is undeniable—and because a great part of our deepest longing is to hold our parents as one in our hearts, as they hold us as the child. We fear it because we have convinced ourselves that the love is not there, or wasn't good enough. We avoid the pain of feeling the longing, or even deny that there is a longing, being fearful of the disappointment. In essence, this is our greatest sabotage; we fear that the love is not there and deny ourselves the opportunity to discover it and feel it, all the time declaring that it is too difficult and painful to face, thereby keeping ourselves in the numbed state of pain we claim to be so afraid of. This pain of separation becomes our *modus operandi*, every aspect of our life becomes governed by it, and it becomes the compass with which we guide ourselves through life, recreating this pain in many of our relationships and life circumstances, and worst of all, with ourselves. I will use a simple analogy here: Good cars don't come from bad factories. On the totally human level, our parents are God, they are the source of our life, and they are the creator from whence we came. When we reject the life that has been given to us, when we say, "My father was not good enough for me" or "My mother did not love me enough", we are saying that the car factory was a bad one, and therefore the car produced—you—is not good enough. A sobering thought, but a true one. When we reject what is, we reject ourselves. When we reject what was, *we reject life itself.*

In working with people on a personal level, many have come seeking advice, guidance and counselling regarding career and relationships. Often they explain that the thing they are seeking simply eludes them or does not last long, be it prosperity, a loving and stable relationship, a successful career, etc. Most of them have struggled for many years, with little success; even though they have put positive thinking and affirmations, meditation, metaphysical concepts for manifesting into practice, the mysterious way of life remains like a carrot on the end of a long stick. After they recount their difficulties and frustration with not understanding why things aren't working for them, I ask one simple question, "Which of your parents do you not respect?" This question is often met with surprise, sometimes shock, sometimes incredulity and annoyance, but the question is always relevant and truth emerges. If they are not in a place of being able to acknowledge a lack of respect for a parent, I then ask the following questions, "Which of your parents do you feel equal to?" or "Which of your parents do you feel superior to?" Once they have composed themselves, most go into defence and justification and the story that reveals the script of their life is exposed. Once the script is revealed, they ask how any of this is relevant to their current woes and challenges. The simplest answer is, life has been passed to us through our parents and therefore everything we are and hope to become is owing to them. This is an inescapable and undeniable truth. When we look at our parents, realising that they were given life by our grandparents, they in turn by our great-grandparents, and so on back to the beginning of all life—which itself remains a great mystery—most of us perceiving only a part of the great jigsaw of our magical universe, we see that the most precious gift of all, life itself, and the aeons of ancestral experience and evolution, have been given to us by mum and dad. It is to them that we owe everything and when we deny them their rightful place and deny our place as the receiver of such gifts, we deny life, the source of all life and the magical universe.

Submission as the Key to Freedom

Most people, on hearing the word submission, immediately move into resistance. They believe it is something that will weaken them, an act of giving their power away, when in actual fact, as we submit to our destiny, a deep sense of peace washes over us and for the first time in our lives we can tap into our authentic power.

The greatest difficulty with submission occurs when we either perceive our family of origin to have been abusive or where actual abuse has occurred. Even if there has been physical, emotional or sexual abuse, it still does not change the fact that the life we have, and therefore our destiny, is inexorably tied up with, and owing to, our family of origin. This is our life, there is no other, and in this sense, our mother is the one and only one for us; likewise our father is the one and only, it cannot be changed, no matter how much we may resist it. When we can accept that our parents are indeed the 'one and only' we can then make the inner movement of accepting that they are the perfect parents for us. How can a parent who was missing, emotionally or physically, be the perfect one? How can the alcoholic parent be the perfect one? How can an abusive parent be the perfect one? How can the parent who left the family home really be the perfect one for us? How can the parent who died when we were a child be the perfect one? It is quite simple…we are our parents. We inherit their gifts and talents, we inherit their inner knowledge and experience, just as they inherited from their forefathers and foremothers, and our very life is because of them. It is a simple truth.

The act of submitting to our parents means receiving the gift of life fully, as it has been passed down to us, without hesitation, without question. When we do this, we open our hearts to fully receive the blessings of life. Before we do this, we often have to struggle to 'get' what is ours and when we do eventually 'get' the things we see as the blessings of life, it often feels empty or we experience not actually wanting what we thought we wanted. When we are incomplete, then nothing in our life feels complete, not our job or our relationship—all of it carries a sense of something missing; the missing link is being our parent's child, blessed with life.

Take a few moments to experience the meditation at the back of this book. It will allow you to feel a deep and profound connection through your parents to the Source of all love and life, become filled with it and be in awe of it. Jesus said "Honour thy mother and father" because he knew that in order to become a Master Magician he needed to give up all resistance to what is. When we reject our parents, or feel superior to them in some way, we literally say 'no' to the life we have been given and challenge destiny and the order of things, thereby cutting ourselves off from the creative life force of the universe.

Avoiding the 'yes but' trap

Even though many people almost immediately grasp the enormity of the gift of life they have been given by their parents, they still very often fall into the 'yes but' trap. The key to keeping out of the 'yes but' trap is knowing what is our business and what isn't. When we are caught in the 'yes but' trap we are always caught in someone else's business, being presumptuous, which leads to arrogance, either veiled or visible. Arrogance is a difficult word for most of us to relate to as we have an image of the meaning of that word. We see arrogance as being people who are dominant, opinionated people with a sense of superiority. Arrogance has many disguises and it is often lurking alive and well behind the mask of shyness, ingratiation and false modesty. On our path towards living a magical life, we are called upon to be exacting in our honesty to face arrogance and its many disguises, head on. When we acknowledge the life we have been given and accept it without question, we open the floodgates of heaven.

Receiving What is Available, Increasing the Flow

In an ideal world, our parents and partners are able to share with us 100% of their potential love. As you become aware that your own ability to share your love and express your gratitude has been impacted with your response to past hurts, so it is with those who gave you life. When you imagine their lives, trials, tribulations and difficulties, you can move to a place of compassion and understanding. Let us imagine that your parents are only able to give you 20% of their potential love. What most of us do is to claim that the 20% is a shortfall, simply not good enough, and we respond by closing our hearts to them, or judge them for the shortcoming. However, part of living a magical life is submitting to and fully receiving the 20% available. Rather than selling yourself short, this encourages the flow of love towards you. In essence, through your acceptance of what is available, lack of resistance and an attitude of gratitude towards the life you have been given, you open a doorway for more love to flow in. It has been said that we can't change the wind, but we can change how we use the sails and capture the wind available in order to move forward. Even if your parents are deceased, this principle still applies as it is an inner movement that is required.

Forgiveness

Forgiveness, of others and of self, is an essential ingredient for freeing up our energy for more successful manifestation. There are some important things to be aware of when you engage in forgiveness. Ask yourself the following question, "Is it more important for me to have peace or to be right?" It is essential that you spend time with this question and answer it with total honestly. Most of us, if not all of us, want to be right more than have peace, at one time or another, so check your inner sense with an open heart and clarity. The biggest problem with forgiveness is falling into the trap of feigned forgiveness. This occurs because many take the position that it is the 'good' forgiving the 'bad' or the 'right' forgiving the 'wrong'. If this is the inner position, then forgiveness has not truly taken place. Part of forgiveness is seeing yourself and the other as human, therefore not infallible or equal to your own ability to cause harm. Forgiveness, like love, can be defined as the complete and total acceptance of what is. We must be cautious when using the term forgiveness, ensuring that we are not coming from a place of superiority. Through Family Constellation process, we have also seen that strong feelings of hatred are equaled by the depth of love that is held for the other and that resistance is indicative of a deep longing for resolution.

The Soul is inclusive of all things, and equal to all things. As a therapist, I have observed that most of us end up imitating the parents and individuals we least respect. The imitation comes from an inner impulse from the Soul to redress an imbalance through becoming equal to that which is excluded. When working with parents, I often ask them what they think their children may say of them. Surprisingly to most clients, when they are honest, they clearly see a lot of parallels between how they view their own parents and how their children may view them. Apples truly do not fall very far from the tree.

Spiritual Pitfalls

With today's spiritual and more metaphysical ways of thinking, we must be cautious that we don't perceive our spiritual outlook on life as superior to other outlooks. All is equal to the Soul and each tradition and way of thinking has a place that is appropriate for some.

Quite often, we can fall into the trap of viewing our parent's generation as being old-fashioned, limited and restrictive in many ways. However, we can choose to take a realistic look at the truth of this. When we consider humanity's evolution of conscience and consciousness, it is clear to see that each generation has changed and developed in these areas, passing down this growth to the next generation. Since time immemorial, each older generation has had its complaints about the 'youth of today' which is testimony to the fact that each generation moves along the evolutionary path just a notch, seemingly gathering momentum with each passing generation. For those of us who consider ourselves at the forefront of new ways of healing and being, we must remember that it is the work of our parent's generation that laid new foundations for this phenomenal growth to take place. Most of you reading this book are either the children or grandchildren of the children and adults of the Second World War and other events that brought sweeping social changes. Therefore, it behoves us to honour previous generations with both gratitude and humility, for they were the groundbreakers who often paid with their own quality of life for the changes in thinking that we all benefit from today.

Spiritual Arrogance

One sunny Saturday I attended what was titled a Metaphysical Breakfast organised by an alternative lifestyle and metaphysical magazine. After the event, I walked across the car park towards my car and overheard two women complaining rather loudly about a third individual. The overheard part of the conversation that left an impression was, "Who does she think she is, she isn't even spiritual!"

The point of recounting this story is to diminish an illusion that many of us involved with new ways of healing, thinking and being often become trapped in the thought that perhaps there will be a special place for us in heaven once we die, or that our lives will be more blessed by some non-physical spiritual authority simply because we meditate, are healers, therapists, metaphysical teachers or students. For me, spiritual growth is determined by our ability to be equal to, and to accept what is, in other words…to love.

Pitfalls for the Healer and Therapist

In my experience, all therapists and healers involved in their craft have been initially motivated by their own pain and the dysfunction of their families. As therapists and healers, when we are unable to be in right relationship to our families, it is impossible for us to be in right relationship to our clients and students. Most therapists and healers enter into their craft from a position of wanting to make right that which went wrong. Family Constellation work enables us to see the broader picture of healing and our place within the family and opens many doorways for us to experience grace and humility in the process. Once we have submitted to what is, we are then able to approach our clients on an equal footing. For when we are motivated by trying to fix the wrongs of the past in our own families, we will also place ourselves above our clients, often 'knowing what is best' and disempowering them in the process.

None of us is here to heal or save the planet, and neither are we here with a higher divine mission. So why do we heal? Why do we become therapists and teachers? We do so because we feel better about ourselves when we practice our craft. When we are able to be honest with ourselves about our true motivation for working within the healing arts, we then become of greater service to those we are serving. For in doing so, we no longer wish to rescue clients, individuals, planets or nations, we simply honour where they are at this moment in time and lend a hand when it is requested. Additionally, as healers and therapists, once we have become honest about our motivation, we become independent of both the good and the negative opinions of others, simply doing our work because it is in our nature to do so. When we seek approval and release the concept that we are in some way special or different, the essence of who we truly are is better able to shine through the layers of masks that we have created. Being a healer or a therapist does not make us special; indeed, in my observation, it is the most ordinary people on the planet who seem to achieve the extraordinary, for they have not fallen into the trap of seeing themselves as special, but simply do what they do because it is their nature to do so. Gandhi and Nelson Mandela are two examples that come to mind…ordinary men with ordinary problems who achieved extraordinary things.

As therapists and healers it is important that we are mindful of the deception that spiritual glamour can imprison us within. How do we present ourselves to the world? Do we wear clothing styles that become uniforms displaying our healing and spiritual status? Do we insist that particular ways of eating, living and being are more spiritual than others? What is important is to be authentic in everything that we do, to be human, rather than attempting to raise ourselves up above the world that we serve through conformity to ideals and images that are an attempt to tell the world that we are in some way special. One of the contradictions in life is that nonconformity has its own rules regarding conformity to nonconformist ideas. Many believe that if you are a healer, then you are required to conform to vegetarianism or to live a 'simple life'. These are all forms of conformity that are designed to separate ourselves from the world and make us in some way special. That is not a statement about vegetarianism, but a statement about spiritual expectations and conformity, for each must choose their own diet appropriate to their own body.

CHAPTER ELEVEN

CREATING YOUR OWN FAMILY TREE

Now that you have read all of the material in this book, your perception of your family tree will have shifted as you begin to understand that which is truly important in terms of family systems and significant events.

Take a large piece of paper on which to create your Family Constellation Tree, using the symbols below as your guide.

Males ☐   Females ○

Miscarriages (if gender unknown) ◫

With parents or couples, place the man on the left and the woman on the right. Place children below the parents, with the eldest child on the far left.

Example 1

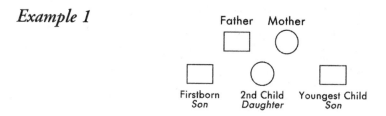

When there has been more than one marriage or a significant relationship prior to marriage to the current parent, place symbols to represent such individuals to the right of the father, or to the left of the mother. Annotate with any significant details.

Example 2

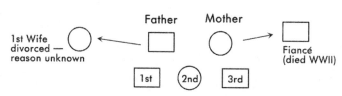

Complete the diagram, going back as many generations as you have information about, including annotations for significant events. Here is a reminder:

- Early death of parents or grandparents
- Accidental deaths, murders, victims of war
- Miscarriages, abortions, stillbirths, infant deaths
- Divorce
- Forced separation of couples owing to racial, religious or other cultural reasons
- Adoptions
- Anyone forced into the role of black sheep or disowned by the family
- Serious illness such as cancer, AIDS, or repeating illness patterns in a family

Once you have completed your Family Constellations Tree, simply look at the map and feel the story of your family through observing your body and your breathing. You may feel a particular emotion or simply be drawn to a part of your Family Constellations Tree.

What is the story? How are you drawn to it?

In meditation, you may wish to ponder this part of your family story, imagining that you are speaking to the individuals involved. Make use of the following healing sentences, feeling the one that is most appropriate:

"Dear _____, it is a pity that you left so early, because we've all missed you."

"Dear _____, even though you died so young, please smile upon me kindly as I live my life fully."

"Dear _____, you were once forgotten, I now take you fully as my _____, and give you a place in my heart."

"Dear _____, although you suffered greatly, I will live my life fully in honour of you."

"Dear _____, one day we shall be together. I shall come when it is my proper time, and not one moment before. Smile upon me kindly if I stay."

These are just a few examples of healing movements that you can start without the assistance of either attending a workshop or working with a practitioner privately.

MEDITATION

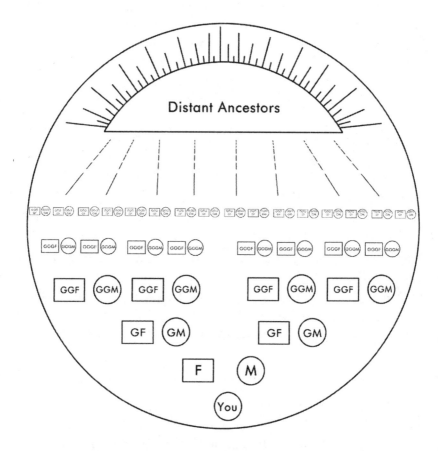

GGGF: Greatgreat Greatgrandfather   GGF: Great Grandfather
GGGM: Greatgreat Grandmother   GGM: Great Grandmother
GF: Grandfather   GM: Grandmother   F: Father   M: Mother
CH: Child

Imagine that your parents are standing behind you, your father behind your right shoulder, your mother behind your left shoulder. Place their parents behind them in similar fashion. Add your great-grandparents behind them, plus another generation and yet another. Keep seeing row upon row of family generations extending out from behind you as if you are the tip of a flat triangle that fans out, back into the mists of time.

Allow this vast crowd to grow and grow, adding generation after generation in your mind's eye until eventually you see the beginning of all life, the source, that original spark. It is still a mystery, but you may wish to call this God or simply "The Source".

Just sit for a moment and feel the strength of support coming from this vast crowd of ancestors, each one having passed the gift of life on to the following generation. Now imagine that you are turning 180 degrees in order to face your parents. Look over their shoulders at this vast crowd and in your mind's eye scan each of the generations as far back as you can go, allowing yourself to feel their richness of experience. Each generation endured hardships, created triumphs and laid the foundations for future development for the next generation. Embrace the knowledge of how all of these ancestors grew in mind, heart and spirit through the passage of time, each generation having opened doorways to new ways of being, doing and thinking for the next generation. Now look at your parents and realise how all of this evolution, wisdom and learning has been given to you as a gift of life by the two very special people standing in front of you, your parents.

Now bow to your parents and your ancestors, inwardly feeling the gratitude for life.

You may do this meditation as often as you feel drawn to. For your convenience, this guided meditation is available on CD, which includes beautiful relaxing music... available from www.familyconstellations.net.

How to attend a workshop

If you are moved to experience this healing work firsthand, please visit www.familyconstellations.net or e-mail the South African Institute for Family Constellations at familyconstellations@telkomsa.net and ask for an international schedule of events including the USA, South Africa and other countries. Requests from those wishing to host a workshop in their area are also gladly received.

For workshops in Johannesburg, South Africa, please call The South African Institute for Family Constellations at The Life Strategy Centre: (011) 614 0821; International +27-11-614 0821.

THE KNOWING FIELD

The term 'the Knowing Field' was initially coined by Dr. Albrecht Mahr in 1997 at the first International Conference on Family Constellations in Wiesloch near Heidelberg in his keynote lecture entitled: "Wisdom does not come to those who sit back: on the use of technique and 'being guided' in family constellations." He and others were deeply impressed by the richness of knowledge emerging in family constellations. The term "Knowing field" seemed to be the most appropriate term for describing the field phenomena which were informing and guiding us in family constellations.

On the one hand it can be seen as a poetic term, poetry being the most accurate language at the level of the soul. On the other hand, "knowing field" is inspired by Rupert Sheldrake's findings on morphogenic fields and extended mind, as well as by quantum physics and its surprising discoveries regarding the transmission of information and knowledge through quantum fields.

ABOUT JOHN PAYNE

John L. Payne is an internationally known and recognised metaphysical teacher, author, healer and Family Constellations Practitioner. He has developed his own style with his work, which is built on unwavering truth and unbridled compassion. Having given more than 100 Family Constellations workshops on four continents, he brings a wealth of experience and knowledge to this work that offers participants and readers alike a clarity that is both healing and supportive.

John is based in Johannesburg, South Africa, and regularly offers workshops in the USA and other locations worldwide. For more information regarding John's schedule or to extend invitations to bring his work your area, please visit www.familyconstellations.net.

ALSO BY JOHN PAYNE

Omni Reveals the Four Principles of Creation

An inspiring and compelling collection of questions and answers are posed to 'Omni', a non-physical group entity channeled through John Payne. Omni is primarily concerned with communicating the four principles of creation which form the core of his teachings, all centering around the idea that the creative aspect of the universe is a natural part of our being.

Throughout the book Omni relates an all encompanning message which states that all is okay with humanity—we are evolving without encountering the prophesied disasters—and will continue to be OK as we gently unfold our potential.

172 pages paperback, ISBN 1-899171-88-6
available from your local bookshop, or from *www.findhornpress.com*